# Low Maintenance

# Low Maintenance

Essential know-how and expert advice for gardening success

# CONTENTS

# WHERE TO START?

There are many easy ways to keep outdoor maintenance to a minimum, although you will need to do a few jobs now and again, just as you would to keep a house clean and tidy. Learning about the conditions in your yard will allow you to choose plants adapted to thrive there, saving you time and money spent on planting replacements. And by planning carefully how you want to use your outdoor space, you can ensure it suits your needs, as well as the time you have available to care for it.

# WHAT IS A LOW-MAINTENANCE YARD?

Reducing the care needed to keep your outdoor space looking its best is easy when you know how. Planning ahead is the key to success, and making time to familiarize yourself with the plants and features that require little maintenance will pay dividends, enabling you to design a space that you can manage with ease. Fortunately, gardens filled with beautiful plants are among the easiest to care for.

**Beds packed** with perennial plants and small shrubs suppress weed growth and are surprisingly easy to maintain.

**Trees and perennial plants,** such as ferns, that perform year after year need only low levels of care.

## REDUCING GARDENING TASKS

While it is possible to keep maintenance to a minimum, any outdoor environment will need some care from time to time, just like a room indoors. Even if you were to pave over your whole yard, it would still need sweeping regularly and the occasional scrub to remove stains. However, there are some features that require more care than others. New gardeners may be surprised to learn that many plants do not come top of that list, and some need almost no annual maintenance provided that they are sited correctly and their roots are well established. A small ornamental tree or compact shrub, for example, may require less work from you to care for than a patio. Add a few flowering perennials, which die down in the winter and pop up again the following spring, and you can create a space that will be the envy of your neighbours while taking only a few days of your time each year. On the other hand, a neat lawn will need mowing every week in summer, which can be a huge task if it covers most of your outdoor space.

## WHY YARDS NEED PLANTS

The common perception of a low-maintenance yard is one where plants are restricted in number and size, but without plenty of leaves and flowers an outdoor space can look barren and unwelcoming. A balance of hard surfaces and planting will create a more beautiful environment, without loading you with work. Trees, shrubs, and other plants are also good for the environment because they absorb carbon dioxide—one of the greenhouse gases responsible for climate change—and help soak up rainwater during storms, thereby reducing flooding around your home.

Research also shows that being in a leafy green space helps us relax and unwind. A little gardening is good for your physical well-being, too—helping to tone muscles and improve fitness. However, time constraints or physical impairments mean that many people are looking for all of these benefits without too much graft—and this is possible when you know how.

**A balance** of hard surfaces and plants is the best option for a beautiful, easy-care garden that also enhances well-being.

**All potted plants** will need to be watered regularly during the growing season, even after it has rained.

## ESSENTIAL CARE

There are some tasks that you will need to make time for, however easy your yard is to maintain. Planting is usually a once- or twice-a-year job, but when plants are mature, many require very little aftercare and will grow for years before they need to be replaced.

Watering new plants in dry weather until they are established is another essential job, and plants in pots will require regular watering from late spring to early fall. You will also need to make time for weeding, especially while your plants are taking root, but there are many ways to reduce weed growth to minimize your workload, and you will find tips throughout this book on easy methods of doing this. If you want a lush lawn, mowing will probably be your most time-consuming task, so ensure you can fit it into your schedule.

Some plants require only occasional pruning, while others may need to be cut once a year to keep them in peak condition. Using easy-care shrubs and trees that comfortably fit your space will also reduce the need to prune.

## GOOD LOOKS

Low-maintenance gardening does not mean that you have to compromise on the look of your outdoor space. A garden filled with permanent plants that

offer seasonal flowers, a small tree to afford some natural shade in summer, and an easy-clean seating area can be yours with just a little annual care.

The key to success is careful planning and taking time initially to get to know your soil, the amount of sun your space receives, and the type of plants that are adapted to thrive in those conditions, all of which will reduce your workload as well as saving you money by avoiding expensive mistakes. Selecting paving or decking that won't show the dirt will reduce maintenance, while using other plants instead of a lawn (see pp.108–109) will bring color and texture into your yard without regular mowing.

**Outdoor spaces** can be very beautiful and easy to tend if you take the time to get to know your garden conditions.

# ASSESSING YOUR NEEDS

**Your yard is a valuable asset, providing an outdoor space in which to entertain, relax, and play, so it's worth spending some time deciding exactly how you want to use it. Whether you are keeping the existing layout or changing the design, careful planning will be needed to ensure that any work you do will have the desired effect, and that your time constraints make your new ideas viable.**

**Composite decking** for a dining area is an easy-care flooring solution if you are prepared to power-wash it annually.

**Slow-growing yew hedging** and a powder-coated metal bench create a low-maintenance secluded seating area.

## TOP PRIORITIES

When planning your low-maintenance space, the first step is to consider who will be using it and how. For example, your priorities may include a space for dining and entertaining, with a safe area for children to play. Features and plants that draw in wildlife such as birds and bees may also be important to you. Make a wish list and set out your aims in order of importance. This will help you prioritize the spaces needed for each activity and to assess whether you can fit them all in. Remember to also include practical necessities, such as a shed for tools and bikes and an area for storing garbage cans.

## TIME IS OF THE ESSENCE

Once you have compiled your wish list, think about how much time you want to spend gardening. For example, you may have a couple of hours each week for mowing the lawn, but no time for much else; or you may feel that watering a couple of herb pots each week in summer and a few days' tidying and pruning in spring or fall is all you can commit to. Whatever your time constraints, you can create a space that will suit your lifestyle once the initial preparation and planting are done. Being realistic at this early stage ensures that you do not waste time and money on plants that you cannot care for easily.

**Drought-tolerant** herbs and flowers will only need watering a couple of times a week, even at the height of summer.

## CHOOSING A STYLE

To get the look you have in mind for your easy-care plot, consider which styles you like best. With the right materials and plant selection, almost any style can be adapted to require minimum maintenance. For example, if you want a neat and tidy space, you could select a patio with pavers in a shade that will disguise dirt, some square or rectangular flowerbeds, and shrubs and perennials with pleasing natural shapes that won't need clipping or staking. Alternatively, you may be aiming for a flowery, wildlife-friendly haven with gravel paths cutting through curved beds. Again, easy-care shrubs and perennials will provide a permanent framework, and to achieve the look you could supplement these with plants that have free-flowing outlines, such as wispy grasses and lax-stemmed flowers that spill over on to a path or patio.

**Leaving the grass** to grow beneath trees creates a romantic seating area in an easy-care, wildlife-friendly yard.

## MAKING PLANS

While some people may not wish to completely redesign their outside space, others will be happy to start again and reconfigure their whole yard to suit their needs. Whichever category you fall into, think about the financial implications and remember that plants as well as materials can be expensive, especially trees and large shrubs, so make sure you factor in these costs as well as the labor required.

If you just want to amend what you have, identify the features that need excessive maintenance and look through this book for alternative options. If the lawn is taking too much time to mow every week or two, would another hard-wearing surface be more practical? For example, a deep layer of bark chips will require almost no maintenance for

a wide path in a natural setting or for an area under play equipment, where it will offer better cushioning than grass, too.

Another task that could become a problem is pruning, especially if shrubs or trees in skinny borders are edged by a path and need cutting back every few months to keep the route clear. One solution would be to move the path and make the border wider while retaining the shrubs and trees. The plants can then grow more naturally without pruning and also offer a beautiful habitat for wildlife. For more detailed advice on designing your space, see pp.14–15.

**TOP TIP** A SLOW-GROWING HEDGE SUCH AS YEW CAN BE CLIPPED ONCE EVERY TWO YEARS IF YOU'RE HAPPY WITH A SLIGHTLY SHAGGY LOOK, AND MAY NEED NO MORE CARE THAN A PAINTED FENCE.

**Moving a path** can save time pruning back shrubs and trees that overhang it, leaving them to grow more naturally.

# GETTING TO KNOW YOUR YARD

Soil may look like dirt to the untrained eye, but it is the most important material in the yard, sustaining both plants and an army of tiny creatures and microorganisms that hold the key to all life on Earth. Testing your soil will help you match up plants suited to it. Assessing where the sun falls and for how long will guide your choices, too, saving you time and money on expensive mistakes.

**Grasses, red valerian, and salvia** are sun-loving perennial plants that will thrive in free-draining sandy soils.

## UNDERSTANDING YOUR SOIL

Not all soils are the same, and different types behave in different ways. Most soils are rich in either sand or clay particles, while some may have similar proportions of both, and are known as loam. Whatever your soil type, there are plants that will thrive in your yard, but it is important to find out which you have so you can match them up (see *opposite*).

Sandy soils consist of relatively large particles, just like the grains on a beach. Water drains easily through the spaces between the particles, which makes these soils dry. They also tend to be infertile because plant nutrients, which are held in a solution of water, are also washed away. Sandy soil is known as "light," not because it weighs less than other types but because it is easy to dig.

Clay soil is made up of tiny particles that hold on to water and plant nutrients. These dense soils are prone to waterlogging in winter and often form hard, cracked surfaces in dry summers. Clay soils are known as "heavy" because they are difficult to dig, but despite their problems, they are fertile and many plants thrive in them.

**Plant nutrients** are dissolved in the water in the soil, which is why moist clay soils tend to be fertile.

**Use a soil testing kit** to determine whether your soil is acid, alkaline, or neutral and which plants will like it.

## THE ACID TEST

The acidity or alkalinity of a soil is known as its pH value. Some plants, such as rhododendrons and camellias, will only grow well on acid soils, while others, including lavender and rock roses, prefer alkaline conditions. Many plants are not too fussy, and catalogs often specify pH needs only when a plant is particularly demanding. You may find acid-loving plants listed as lime-hating or lime-intolerant. Kits for testing pH are easy to use, and it is well worth assessing the soil in a few areas of your yard to check whether it is acid, alkaline, or neutral.

## CHECKING YOUR SOIL TYPE

To determine which type of soil you have, dig up a small sample from just below the surface, leave it to dry off a little if wet, and roll it between your fingers.

**SANDY SOIL** When rolled between the fingers, sandy soil feels gritty, and when damp it will fall apart when you try to mold it into a ball or sausage shape. It is also generally pale in color.

**CLAY SOIL** Smooth and dense, clay soil retains its shape when molded into a sausage shape or ball. Soils with a very high clay content will not crack even when bent into a horseshoe shape.

## IMPROVING YOUR SOIL

Although there are plants that will be happy in your soil whatever type you have, you can widen your choices by improving the conditions. The best way to make a very free-draining, infertile, sandy soil more moisture retentive, or a heavy waterlogged clay more manageable, is to add organic matter such as well-rotted garden compost or manure from an organic source. Apply a 2 in (5 cm) layer over the soil in the fall if you have clay, or in spring if you have sand—either season will work if you have loam. Worms and other creatures will bring the organic matter down into the soil where it binds clay particles into larger aggregates, creating bigger spaces between them for water to drain through. In sandy soils, the added compost coats the sand particles in a dark substance known as "humus," helping them retain more water and plant nutrients.

**Spreading compost or manure,** known as mulch, over the soil will improve both heavy clays and free-draining sands.

## HERE COMES THE SUN

Checking how much sun your yard receives will help you choose the right plants for your plot. Some plants thrive in full sun, others prefer shade, and if you grow either in the wrong light conditions they may not perform well and could even die. When grown in poor light, plants that enjoy bright sun will become tall and leggy as their stems stretch toward the light, while plants that prefer shade will scorch when grown in too much sun.

To find out how much sun your garden receives, stand with your back to the house and use a compass. If you are facing south, the garden will receive sun for most of the day in summer; if the compass points north, your plot will be shady. Those facing east or west will receive the most sun in the morning or evening respectively. Remember, too, that trees and buildings will cast shade in an otherwise sunny plot.

**Take pictures** from a top-floor window to see where the sun falls on your yard at different times of the day and year.

# DESIGNING FOR LOW MAINTENANCE

The design of your space, as well as your choice of plants, can determine its maintenance needs, and making a few changes to your existing layout could save you time. Wide paths and generous patios edged with beds of easy-care plants are good options, while reducing the size of a lawn will immediately cut your workload. Installing an accessible outside faucet is another way to save time when watering.

**Checking the heights** and spreads of plants will ensure they fit your beds when fully grown and won't need cutting back.

## SHAPING UP YOUR SPACE

Having assessed your needs and prioritized which features and areas of the yard are most important to you (see pp.10–11), start planning what will go where. A dining area close to the house will be convenient for serving food, but if it is shaded, you may also want a seating area in a sunny spot farther away. Check that any patio is large enough to accommodate your furniture. Measure your dining set and ensure there is about 4 ft (1.2 m) of space around it so guests do not have to walk across grass or flowerbeds to access the chairs. This will prevent bald patches from forming on the lawn and trampled plants in beds that will need to be frequently replaced. The materials you use will also have an impact on maintenance (see pp.100–101).

Geometric-shaped lawns are easier to maintain than complex shapes—trimming a serpentine edge will take twice as long as maintaining a straight or gently curved line. An easy way to create a crisp, designer look that's easy to care for is to use bold, simple shapes for your lawn and paved areas, and fill the spaces between with planting. Avoid narrow beds, which will restrict you to a limited choice of tiny plants.

**Installing a brick edging** that is slightly lower than the grass will make the task of mowing quicker and easier.

## EASY ACCESS

Planning the access through the yard is important, especially for paths edged with planting. Make your main path wide enough to allow space for plants to arch over it without blocking the route and for a wheelbarrow to transport lawn clippings and garden waste. A width of at least 3 ft (1 m) is advisable for most spaces, even small plots. Also consider how a path will connect to a shed that houses the mower and your tools—you don't want to haul the mower through a narrow, winding path to the lawn, adding yet more time to its maintenance. Make sure, too, that all the seating areas are easily connected to the house, so you can bring out food and drinks without walking across the grass.

**Wide paths** allow easy access for a wheelbarrow to transport heavy plants and remove garden waste.

## WATER HOT SPOTS

An outside faucet is a must for any low-maintenance space, so if you do not have one already, call in a qualified plumber to install a water supply in a convenient spot. If you can, invest in one or two rain barrels to attach to the downspout on your house, as well as to any structure such as a shed or outdoor office. Not only will they harvest a free water supply, they can also be invaluable in a larger yard. Creating new flowerbeds and a vegetable patch close to a barrel will make them easier to water when the young plants are establishing, while grouping plants in pots and containers close to a barrel or faucet will also reduce the time and effort needed to water them.

> **TOP TIP** IN A SLOPING YARD, MAKE A FLOWERBED AT THE BOTTOM OF THE HILL SO THAT RAINWATER DRAINS INTO IT, REDUCING THE NEED FOR WATERING. IF THE AREA IS PRONE TO FLOODING, ADD SOME OTHER PLANTS OR A TREE FURTHER UP THE SLOPE TO ABSORB THE EXCESS WATER DURING AND AFTER HEAVY RAIN.

**Mark out circular beds or lawns** on the ground using string and temporary marking spray paint.

## MEASURING

Creating a simple plan of your yard is one of the best ways of checking what will fit where. Using a long tape measure, note the length and width of your plot, and the two diagonal measurements across it. Use these to draw up a paper or digital plan to scale; for example, 3 ft (1 m) on the ground could equal 1 in (2 cm) on your plan. You can then see more clearly how much space you have for patios, play areas, paths, and flowerbeds. Then mark out your areas on the ground, using a temporary marking spray paint or string stretched between posts.

**Summer pots** filled with flowers will be easier to water if placed close to an outdoor water supply.

**Drought-tolerant shrubs** and perennial plants will flower year after year in free-draining soil that receives plenty of sunshine.

# LOW-MAINTENANCE PLANTING

**Your choice of easy-care plants that take little time to maintain will largely depend on the conditions in your space. Trees, shrubs, and flowers that perform year after year will reduce time spent planting, while matching their needs to the available sunlight and soil in the yard will allow them to thrive with very little intervention from you. Beds and borders packed with the plants you love will also reduce the numbers of those you don't, such as weeds.**

# PLANTS EXPLAINED

From towering trees to ground-hugging herbs, plants come in all shapes and sizes, and each uses a range of strategies to survive. Some long-lived species with tough, woody stems can live for decades, while other plants produce copious seeds each year to ensure their longevity. The best choices for low-maintenance gardening are enduring plants that need little intervention to perform well year after year, so it's useful to know which are which. Learning about how different plants grow and reproduce will also enable you to choose the best for your specific circumstances.

**Shrubs, perennials, annuals, and grasses** mingle in this bed to produce a riot of summer color.

**Annual bedding plants** provide a long season of summer color but need to be planted every year in late spring.

## CHOOSING PLANTS

Plants fall into a few main groups, such as trees and shrubs, many of which you will be familiar with. However, you may not be aware of how their growth habits can determine the time and effort needed to maintain them. While most plants require more care when they are young, the workload for some, including shrubs and perennial plants (see *opposite*), will fall dramatically once they are mature and their roots are established. Taking time to choose plants suited to your conditions (see *pp.12–13*) will also ensure they thrive with little help from you.

## CHECK PLANT LABELS

It's easy to be seduced by the beautiful flowers on display at the garden center or splashed across the pages of a nursery website or catalog, but take a moment to consider whether the plants that catch your eye are right for you. Check the plant labels or descriptions online for final heights and spreads to ensure you can fit them into your plot. This information will also help you site them in an appropriate spot and avoid costly mistakes; for example, a shrub that looks like a few small twigs when you buy it in spring may grow to a height and spread of 6 ft (2 m) or more after a couple of years, so planting it at the front of a bed could be a problem. Labels also specify a plant's soil and light needs, together with other details, such as its value to pollinators.

**Check labels** for plants' final heights and spreads, as well as the soil and light conditions they require.

# IDENTIFYING DIFFERENT PLANT TYPES

**ANNUALS AND BIENNIALS** Plants that germinate, flower, set seed, and die all in one year are known as "annuals." Hardy annuals will withstand frost, while tender types won't tolerate low temperatures. Many summer bedding plants are tender annuals and need to be planted every year. "Biennials" germinate and form stems and leaves in the first year, then flower, set seed, and die in the second year. They can also be hardy or tender.

**PERENNIALS, GRASSES, AND FERNS** Perennial plants live for many years, but the leaves, stems, and flowers of most die down in winter before new growth emerges the following spring. A few perennials retain their leaves in winter. Grasses can be deciduous or evergreen and behave like perennials, while most bamboos are evergreen. Ferns can also be evergreen or deciduous and live for many years. The hardy plants in this category are easy to care for, but avoid vigorous bamboos that spread rapidly.

**BULBS** Plants that form bulblike structures, including corms, tubers, and rhizomes, as well as true bulbs, fall into this category. They include spring-flowering tulips and daffodils, which are planted in the fall, and summer-flowering dahlias, lilies, and gladioli, which are planted in spring. While hardy types will die down after flowering and pop up the following year with no intervention, others are tender and may need to be protected from the cold indoors during winter.

**SHRUBS** These woody-stemmed plants can be deciduous or evergreen, and the hardy types will help create a permanent framework in the space. Shrubs range from ground-hugging plants, such as thymes and heather, to those with treelike proportions, so check heights and spreads carefully before buying. Many also flower and some produce decorative berries and colorful fall foliage. Most shrubs are very easy to maintain.

**CLIMBERS** These woody-stemmed or perennial plants can be evergreen or deciduous, tall or short, and they use a variety of methods to climb. Twining types, such as clematis, use leaf stalks, tendrils, or stems to coil around a support; the thorny stems of roses act as hooks to heave themselves up; and self-clinging climbers, including Virginia creeper and ivy, employ adhesive pads or aerial roots. Some climbers are easy to maintain once established.

**TREES** Providing height and shade in the garden, trees can be evergreen or deciduous, large or small. The canopies of trees can be spreading, rounded, conical, or weeping in shape, so check these details, which will determine where to site them. Trees can also offer flowers, ornamental bark, and foliage interest, and some are almost maintenance-free once established, but will need regular watering when young.

**MARGINALS AND AQUATIC PLANTS** Plants that thrive in water fall into the following categories: "marginals," which grow in shallow water; "aquatic plants," including water lilies, that generally grow at depths of 12–36 in (30–90 cm); and "oxygenators," which are submerged, fast-growing plants that can help keep the water clear. Not all water plants are suitable for yards or easy to maintain, so check the guidance on pp.118–121 before buying.

**Annual plants include petunias** such as 'Frenzy Blue Vein'.

**The Iran tulip *Tulipa urumiensis*** is an easy-care spring bulb.

**Water lilies such as *Nymphaea* 'Indiana'** are aquatic plants.

# BASIC PRINCIPLES

The key to creating beautiful beds and borders that require little annual maintenance is to use plants that are adapted to thrive in your space. Assessing your conditions (*see pp.12–13*) will provide you with the tools to draw up a list of plants that not only have visual appeal but also suit your site and soil. Planting in spring or fall can also save you watering them, as rain usually falls more frequently in these seasons, allowing nature to do the work for you. Also reduce time and effort by making sure that large plants will fit their allocated space when mature to avoid having to move them.

**Lavender, scabious,** and rose campion (*Lychnis coronaria*) are easy-care perennials for a sunny site and free-draining soil.

**Rhododendrons** make a spectacular statement in spring but will only thrive in acid soil.

## RIGHT PLANT, RIGHT PLACE

The rule of thumb that all professional gardeners are taught is to select the right plant for the right place, which basically means matching species that are adapted to the conditions in the space. Start by selecting your favorites from the planting suggestions on pp.26–33, and, if you have space, also select one or more trees (see pp.40–47), along with a few smaller plants for the shady areas beneath them. Check that your soil matches the conditions the plants on your list enjoy, then divide the list into those that like sun and the shade-lovers, with a third column for plants that will cope with either. Narrowing down your plant choices will help you make the right decisions, selecting only those that will thrive with little aftercare once established.

## PLANNING FOR SIZE

Armed with your plant wish list, now note the heights and spreads of each one. Their size will determine their position in the border: the largest plants will need to be at the back, so that they do not cast shade or block the view of others. Place large shrubs and trees first, then the smaller plants in front, checking that they all have enough space to grow.

Make your beds and borders as large as possible—a minimum width of 3 ft (1 m) is a good marker. Wide beds allow you to include a range of plants that perform at different times of the year, while very narrow beds often provide space for just one type of plant, potentially leaving you with a dull clump of leaves after it has finished flowering.

**Check that you have space** for large shrubs such as this *Viburnum plicatum*.

The **flower spikes** of this pink salvia contrast well with the rounded blooms of the blue hardy geranium.

## SHAPES AND COLORS

To create a beautiful effect, match up the shapes and colors of different plants, contrasting tall flower spikes such as those of salvias with flat-topped plants like sedums (*Hylotelephium*) or the round blooms of hardy geraniums. If you are not sure what effect some of the plants on your list will produce, visit a garden center or nursery regularly so you can see them at various stages of growth before buying. Remember that foliage lasts longer than flowers, so try to put together a collection of plants with contrasting or matching leaf shapes and colors, too.

## SEASONAL SUCCESS

Year-round color is often top of people's list of priorities for their space. One solution is to pack your plot with evergreens, but this can create a boring and static scene. Deciduous shrubs and trees may lose their leaves in winter, but this often reveals a beautiful network of stems after they fall, and the flowers and blossom that follow in spring can be breathtaking, too. While you may have to rake fall leaves from a lawn, leaving them on your beds will actually help protect and nourish the soil, as well as cut your workload. The best effects can be achieved with a mix of easy-care evergreens and deciduous woody plants, with perennials that provide flowers in spring, summer, and fall woven in between.

You can also squeeze in spring bulbs under trees or between perennials, creating a burst of early seasonal color while many plants are just poking through the soil. The foliage of bulbs can also shade the soil and help suppress weed-seed germination, saving you weeding later in the season.

The **bronze stems** of Tibetan cherry create a focal point all year, especially in winter when the leaves have fallen.

## POT FACTS

One myth that has fooled many novice gardeners is that plants in pots are easier to maintain than those in flowerbeds. Nothing could be further from the truth. Plants that are grown in the soil create extensive root networks that can tap into water and nutrients deep in the ground, sustaining them even during periods of drought. Plants in pots, on the other hand, rely on you to deliver nearly all of their water and nutrient requirements, which means frequent watering and feeding. If you do want a few pots, choose plants that are easy to maintain (see pp.80–89).

**Plants in pots** are more time-consuming to maintain than those grown in the ground.

### NEED TO KNOW

- Easy-care perennial plants that die down in winter and reappear each spring look effective when planted in groups of three or more of the same type.
- Check plants' final sizes and give them room to spread, filling any gaps initially with annuals, which will provide extra color and help suppress weed growth.
- Alternatively, plant perennials more closely together, so their foliage covers the soil and shades out the weeds. You may then have to move some of them in a few years, but this could take less time than weeding.

# CREATING EASY-CARE BORDERS

The best time to create a new bed or border is in early fall or early spring, which are the ideal seasons for planting. If you're including drought-loving Mediterranean-style species, such as lavender and rock roses, plant your bed in spring to prevent the young plants dying in cold, wet soil. You can carve out a new bed in a day, and preparing it well at the start lays the foundations for less work later on.

**Deep borders** allow you to create a long, seasonal display of easy-care perennials such as sedums and grasses.

**This border creates a beautiful foliage effect** with shade-loving sweet box and pulmonaria, together with irises and helichrysum in the sunny spots.

## LOCATING YOUR BORDER

Having assessed your site and put together a list of the plants you want to grow (see pp.12–13 and pp.20–21), next consider where would be the best spot to make your bed or border. If you are updating an existing bed, check that it has the right amount of sun or shade for your chosen plants—you may find that by simply making it a little bigger, you will be able accommodate more of those you love.

For a new planting space, choose an area that offers either a combination of full sun (sun for at least six hours a day in summer) and an area in a little shade, which will suit the widest range of plants, or make two or more beds to accommodate your wish list. A sunny site will dry out quickly, so you will have to water new plants more frequently while they establish than those in shade. With this in mind, think about your water sources and how easy it will be to irrigate the new bed (see pp.130–131).

Other spots where initial watering will be essential are under trees and areas beside fences, walls, and hedges. Leave a gap of 18–24 in (45–60 cm) unplanted around them, and cover with a mulch (see opposite) where the soil is driest.

## MARKING THE SITE

Large geometrically shaped beds and borders are the easiest to maintain, as they will allow space for your plants to grow without encroaching on lawns, patios, and pathways. Use string pulled taut between canes to mark out rectangles and squares, or plant a cane in the center of a proposed circular bed, attach string the length of the radius required and use it like a compass to mark out the shape. Use the same technique or lay down a garden hose to define a sweeping curve. Dig around the edges of the bed or border with a sharp spade, removing sod as you go if you are cutting it out of a lawn.

**Use a garden hose** as a guide to mark out a border with a sweeping curve–shaped outline.

> **TOP TIP** INSTALL STEPPING-STONES MADE FROM LOGS FROM PRUNED TREES OR OLD PAVERS THROUGH A LARGE BORDER TO ALLOW ACCESS TO ALL AREAS FOR ANNUAL MAINTENANCE WITHOUT YOU TRAMPLING ON PRECIOUS PLANTS OR THE SOIL— REGULAR FOOTFALL WILL SQUEEZE OUT THE AIR YOUR PLANTS NEED TO THRIVE.

## MULCHING MATTERS

Whether you have clay or sandy soil, an organic mulch will help improve it (see p.13), and you can add one to your bed after a period of rain or once you have watered the soil thoroughly. Choose from well-rotted manure, a proprietary soil conditioner, leaf mold, or garden compost. You can purchase these materials in bulk or in large bags at garden centers and home improvement stores. You will need a layer of 2 in

(5 cm) or a little deeper to cover the bed, and it can be applied before you add the plants or afterward. If you apply a mulch beforehand, push back the material, dig a planting hole in the soil, and then replace the mulch when the plant is in place, leaving a small gap around the stems of shrubs and trees.

**Apply a mulch** about 2 in (5 cm) deep around your plants and wash your hands thoroughly after handling it.

## PREPARING THE SOIL

Once you have created the outline of the bed, check the condition of the soil. Yards of new-build homes are often used as dumping grounds for bricks and other construction materials, so if your spade hits these obstacles, dig them out before planting. This may mean that you have to import some topsoil to fill the gaps, which will help get your new plants off to a good start. You can buy topsoil from garden centers and home improvement stores.

In any yard, new or mature, you will probably find large stones, fallen twigs or branches, and other debris, which will need to be removed from the bed or border before you start planting. Natural materials such as twigs and leaves can be piled up in a quiet corner of the yard, perhaps beside a fence or wall, and left to make a home for wildlife—they will also gradually decompose and enrich the soil. Remove pernicious weeds such as dandelions, bindweed, and docks, roots and all. If you have not already checked your soil type, now is the time to do it (see pp.12–13) to double check that your plants match your conditions.

**Remove thistles** and other large weeds from the bed by hand, digging out as many of the roots as possible.

# PLANTING A BED OR BORDER

Having purchased your favorite plants, it is time to start installing them—but before you put a spade in the ground, set them out to make sure you're happy with their positions. Each will need space to grow to its full potential without overshadowing or out-competing its neighbors. Plant them with care and they will reward you with a beautiful display that should grow and flower unaided once established.

**After a year** these easy-care plants should need very little care apart from watering during severe droughts.

## WHAT TO PLANT WHERE

Whether you are designing a new bed or adding to an old one, group your plant purchases according to their type and final sizes by checking the details on the labels. Then water them thoroughly before placing each group in order on your bed, setting them out while still in their pots to check that you are happy with the final composition. Consider the placement of any trees first: make sure that they will not cast too much shade over the bed, unless you are planning a woodland theme. Next, set out the shrubs, positioning them for maximum impact and seasonal interest (see also pp.20–21), while ensuring that the tallest are behind shorter plants. Shrubs are generally planted singly, but you can use a row of small ones to edge a bed or pathway.

Finally, place the perennials and annuals, which can be woven in between the shrubs. Plant later-flowering types, even if they are slightly taller, in front of the earlier flowers (those that bloom before midsummer). This placement means that as the early blooms die down and their leaves start to look a bit tattered, plants that flower later, whose leaves will still be in prime condition, will cover them up.

**Set out your plants** in their pots in your bed to check that they are in the right position before planting.

# PLANTING TO PERFECTION

Once you are happy with the layout of all the plants, you can begin planting. To plant trees, see pp.40–41. For shrubs, perennials, and annuals, dig a hole twice as wide and about the same depth as the root ball—most will prefer to be planted at the same depth as they were in their original pots, so don't be tempted to bury them deeper or leave the roots exposed above the soil surface. A wide hole will allow the roots to expand easily. If the roots of your plants are twining round the edge of the root ball, gently tease them out with your fingers before planting.

You can add some mycorrhizal fungi, available in packets from garden centers and nurseries, to the planting hole. These special fungi help increase the size of the plants' root balls (see also p.133). If you have chosen your plants carefully and they are suitable for your soil, you should not need to include additional fertilizer at this stage. However, if you think your soil is particularly infertile, add a balanced organic fertilizer containing ingredients such as bonemeal or blood, fish, and bone. After planting, gently press down the soil around the roots with your toe to remove large air gaps, and use a hose with a fine spray or a can fitted with a rose head to give each plant a long drink.

**Carefully prise out roots** that have coiled tightly around in the pot to help them grow away into the soil more easily.

# CARING FOR YOUR PLANTS

Water new plants every few days during dry spells until you see fresh leaves and stems emerging. At this point, you can water less frequently, but do not leave them to dry out during their first year. Pay particular attention to new trees and shrubs, which demand plenty of water to sustain their growth during the first two or three years, but then become quite independent and almost maintenance-free. Other easy-care perennial plants or bulbs suggested in this book should be fairly well-established by the second year after planting and will need far less watering or no watering at all, unless you experience a long period of drought in spring or summer.

Most plants in the ground will not need regular feeding either, provided you have chosen them to suit your particular site and soil conditions. In the first few years, reapply an organic mulch each year in the fall, if you have clay soil, or in spring if your soil is sandy. However, as your border becomes more established, it may not need this annual treatment.

If the leaves of plants such as annuals are turning yellow, you could try adding a liquid seaweed fertilizer to see if nutrient deficiency is the cause.

**Give new plants a good soaking** with each watering, targeting the soil over the roots rather than the leaves or flowers.

## NEED TO KNOW

- To reduce the time spent watering new plants, install a seep or soaker hose. These have tiny holes along their length and deliver water slowly to the plants' roots.
- Lay your hoses on the soil around the plants in your bed, and attach them to an automatic timer affixed to an outdoor tap.
- Program your timer to water the plants in the early morning or evening when evaporation rates are at their lowest.
- Cover the hoses with a mulch of seasoned wood chips or organic matter to reduce evaporation rates further, and your new plants should flourish.

# BED AND BORDER PLANTS

When selecting plants for a bed or border, choose a few easy shrubs that will suit your plot. Not only will they create structure and a permanent framework, these woody plants will also provide a leafy backdrop against which flowering perennials and bulbs can shine. Try planting perennials in bold groups of three or more to produce a confection of color as the seasons turn, and weave swathes of spring bulbs in between them to lend another layer of interest earlier in the year. Many shrubs also flower, adding to the seasonal highlights.

## ABELIA *ABELIA*

**HEIGHT AND SPREAD** up to 8 × 8 ft (2.5 × 2.5 m)
**SOIL** Any, except wet
**HARDINESS** Hardy to 5°F (−15°C)
**SUN** ☼

Abelias are useful semi-evergreen shrubs (evergreen in warm climates) with dark green, glossy foliage that is bronze-tinged when young, creating a two-tone effect. The small pink flowers appear from summer to early fall. While some are large plants best kept to the back of a wide border, smaller forms, such as 'Edward Goucher', are more compact, usually reaching just 3–4 ft (1–1.2 m). Planted in a sheltered spot out of drying winds, these plants need little aftercare, apart from an occasional trim.

**Long-lasting pink flowers** decorate 'Edward Goucher' from summer to fall.

## BUTTERFLY BUSH *BUDDLEIA DAVIDII*

**HEIGHT AND SPREAD** up to 8 × 8 ft (2.5 × 2.5 m)
**SOIL** Well drained
**HARDINESS** Fully hardy
**SUN** ☼ ☼

The butterfly bush is an easy-care stalwart, with its large flower heads that attract bees and butterflies from summer to early fall. Choose from white, purple, pink, and dark red flowers, and if space is tight opt for a dwarf cultivar such as one of the Buzz Series, which grow to 4 ft (1.2 m). These drought-tolerant plants rarely need watering, but they benefit from an annual prune in late winter or early spring to encourage new flowering stems. Cut back to 2–3 ft (60–90 cm) from the ground.

**'Nanho Purple'** produces fragrant purple flowers in summer and early fall.

## CALIFORNIA LILAC *CEANOTHUS*

**HEIGHT AND SPREAD** up to 12 × 10 ft (4 × 3 m)
**SOIL** Well drained
**HARDINESS** Hardy to 14°F (−10°C)
**SUN** ☼

Most California lilacs produce clear blue flower heads in late spring. There are also a smaller number of white and pink forms, and a few that bloom in fall. They come in a wide range of sizes, with compact cultivars such as 'Skylark' for small spaces, or the treelike *Ceanothus arboreus* 'Trewithen Blue' for the back of a border. These plants are easy to care for if you have a sunny site and free-draining soil but will fail in heavy clays and shade, so check before buying that you have the right conditions.

***Ceanothus × veitchianus*** produces its deep blue flowers from spring to early summer.

## MEXICAN ORANGE BLOSSOM *CHOISYA*

**HEIGHT AND SPREAD** up to 6 × 6 ft (2 × 2 m)
**SOIL** Well drained
**HARDINESS** Hardy to 10°F (−12°C)
**SUN** ☼ ☀

Mexican orange blossoms are medium to large evergreen shrubs that are very easy to care for. One of the best is *Choisya* × *dewitteana* 'Aztec Pearl', which produces fingerlike foliage and sweetly scented white flowers in late spring, with a second, sparser flush of blooms often appearing in the summer. It performs well without pruning, and remains relatively compact, but any wayward stems can be cut back in early summer. It also withstands drought once established.

**Few shrubs** can beat the Mexican orange blossom 'Aztec Pearl' for year-round impact, with its evergreen foliage and sweetly scented flowers.

## ROCK ROSE *CISTUS*

**HEIGHT AND SPREAD** up to 3 × 3 ft (1 × 1 m)
**SOIL** Well drained
**HARDINESS** Hardy to 14°F (−10°C)
**SUN** ☼

While each papery white or pink bloom lasts just a day, the rock rose bears them in profusion for many weeks over the summer, and the silvery evergreen foliage offers interest all year. This sun-loving shrub thrives in poor, well-drained soil; in colder climates, choose a sheltered spot and try *Cistus* × *argenteus* 'Silver Pink' or *C.* × *hybridus*, which are among the hardiest types. Once established, the rock rose requires no pruning or watering, but it is relatively short-lived and may need replacing after ten years.

**In a sunny garden,** the white flowers of *Cistus* × *hybridus* will appear over many weeks.

## WINGED SPINDLE *EUONYMUS ALATUS*

**HEIGHT AND SPREAD** 5 × 5 ft (1.5 × 1.5 m)
**SOIL** Any, except wet
**HARDINESS** Fully hardy
**SUN** ☼ ☀

This deciduous shrub, known as winged spindle or fire bush, is grown primarily for its dazzling fall colors. In summer, the green foliage and tiny green-white flowers provide a neutral backdrop for other colorful plants, but as temperatures fall, it takes center stage when the leaves turn pink-red and pink fruits with orange seeds appear. Easygoing and drought-tolerant, it needs no regular pruning, but you can remove misplaced stems in late winter. 'Compactus' is a good choice for a small space.

**In the fall,** the leaves of 'Compactus' turn pink-red and the colorful fruits appear.

## WINTER CREEPER *EUONYMUS FORTUNEI*

**HEIGHT AND SPREAD** 24 × 36 in (60 × 90 cm) or more
**SOIL** Any, except wet
**HARDINESS** Fully hardy
**SUN** ☼ ☀

The evergreen winter creeper will sail through long periods of drought or cold weather unscathed, although it may lose a few leaves in especially harsh winters. The cultivar 'Emerald 'n' Gold' is one of the best-known, its yellow and green variegated leaves lighting up a shady spot and outshining the tiny green early summer flowers. Use it to edge a border or for spots of permanent color between seasonal flowering plants. It can be trimmed in late spring, but requires no other care once established.

**Bright foliage** makes 'Emerald 'n' Gold' an invaluable addition to an easy-care yard.

## HARDY FUCHSIA *FUCHSIA MAGELLANICA*

**HEIGHT AND SPREAD** 5 × 5 ft (1.5 × 1.5 m)
**SOIL** Well drained; moist but well drained
**HARDINESS** Hardy to 14°F (−10°C)
**SUN** ☼ ◑

Hardy fuchsias are deciduous shrubs ideal for the back of a border, where their small leaves create a green screen that acts as a foil for colorful spring and summer flowers. As the summer progresses, dainty, often two-tone blooms appear, hanging from the arching stems like pendent earrings. Once established, these shrubs rarely need watering and, on well-drained soils, may be hardy to lower than stated temperatures. If branches die in a cold winter, just cut them down in spring and they will reshoot.

**The pendent flowers** of the hardy fuchsia come in shades of pink, purple, red, and white.

## TREE MALLOW *LAVATERA × CLEMENTII*

**HEIGHT AND SPREAD** 3 × 3 ft (1 × 1 m)
**SOIL** Any, except wet
**HARDINESS** Hardy to 5°F (−15°C)
**SUN** ☼

Tree mallows are drought-tolerant, fast-growing deciduous shrubs, with young plants often reaching their full height within two years. Ideal for the middle to back of a border, 'Barnsley' is one of the prettiest cultivars, its displays of white flowers that age to pale pink appearing throughout the summer, set off by the gray-green lobed leaves. This mallow is also relatively compact, compared to some larger lavatera varieties that can reach over 6 ft (2 m) in height and spread, and rarely requires pruning.

**Large, shimmering,** white and pink flowers appear on 'Barnsley' throughout summer.

## FLAKY JUNIPER *JUNIPERUS SQUAMATA*

**HEIGHT AND SPREAD** Height up to 16 × 39 in (40 × 90 cm)
**SOIL** Well drained
**HARDINESS** Fully hardy
**SUN** ☼ ◑

Most flaky junipers are small, coniferous shrubs with needlelike evergreen foliage, often used for the front of a border or edge of a raised bed. 'Blue Carpet' is a popular cultivar, its spreading stems of steely blue-gray leaves creating a weed-suppressing mat over the soil. Almost maintenance-free once established, these shrubs survive drought and low temperatures, rarely suffer from pests or diseases, and only need a trim when the stems outgrow their allotted space.

**The colorful foliage** of 'Blue Carpet' creates an eye-catching edge to the front of a border.

## NINEBARK *PHYSOCARPUS OPULIFOLIUS*

**HEIGHT AND SPREAD** 5 × 3 ft (1.5 × 1 m)
**SOIL** Moist but well drained
**HARDINESS** Fully hardy
**SUN** ☼ ◑

If you are looking for colorful leaves to decorate your border, ninebark is a great choice. Try the burgundy foliage of the tall 'Diabolo' for the back of a border, or the more compact 'Lady in Red', with its reddish-brown leaves, in a smaller space. The white or pink flowers that appear in late spring are an added bonus. Once established, these deciduous shrubs will tolerate periods of drought and need very little pruning; simply remove unwanted or dead stems at the base in late winter or early spring.

**'Lady in Red'** is a compact form that creates a striking contrast to green-leaved shrubs.

## FLOWERING CURRANT *RIBES SANGUINEUM*

**HEIGHT AND SPREAD** 6 × 5 ft (2 × 1.5 m)
**SOIL** Any, except wet
**HARDINESS** Fully hardy
**SUN** ☼ ☀

In spring, this shrub bears pendent, conical clusters of pink or white blooms on bare stems, creating a colorful focal point at the back of a border. The lobed green foliage appears as the flowers fade and the shrub then offers a neutral backdrop for other flowering plants that perform later. Tolerant of drought and low temperatures, flowering currants are easy to grow and will be happy in full sun or a few hours of shade each day. Simply cut back dead or unwanted branches after flowering in early summer.

**The pink flowers** of the cultivar 'Koja' brighten up the border in spring.

## JAPANESE SPIREA *SPIRAEA JAPONICA*

**HEIGHT AND SPREAD** 24 × 24 in (60 × 60 cm)
**SOIL** Any, except wet
**HARDINESS** Fully hardy
**SUN** ☼ ☀

It's hard to find a low-growing deciduous shrub that offers better value than the Japanese spirea 'Magic Carpet'. The young leaves are orange-red when they open in spring, turn yellow over summer and then fiery red in the fall, while pink flowers add more color in summer. This compact shrub needs no pruning and tolerates periods of drought and cold winters. Use it to weave color through a border and match it with blue and purple flowers. Grow in full sun for the most vivid foliage hues.

**'Magic Carpet'** offers interest from spring to fall with its leaf colors and bright blooms.

## SWEET BOX *SARCOCOCCA*

**HEIGHT AND SPREAD** up to 5 × 6 ft (1.5 × 2 m)
**SOIL** Any, except wet
**HARDINESS** Hardy to 5°F (−15°C)
**SUN** ☀ ☼

Producing a mound of glossy green foliage, these shade-loving evergreen shrubs provide color and structure when planted among spring- and summer-flowering bulbs or perennials. In winter, their tiny, white, highly scented flowers appear, offering a sensory treat at a time when few other plants are at their peak. *Sarcococca confusa* and *S. hookeriana* var. *digyna* are good choices for small spaces, as they take many years to reach their ultimate height. You can also keep them in check by trimming them in early spring.

***Sarcococca hookeriana* var. *digyna*** is a reliable and easy-to-grow evergreen shrub.

## WEIGELA *WEIGELA*

**HEIGHT AND SPREAD** up to 6 × 5 ft (2 × 1.5 m)
**SOIL** Any, except wet
**HARDINESS** Fully hardy
**SUN** ☼ ☀

Weigelas are deciduous shrubs that can grow to be almost treelike or just hip-height, depending on the cultivar, so check plant labels for the size you want. Their main appeal is their long-lasting tubular flowers, available in shades of red, pink, and white, which bloom from spring to summer. Some also sport variegated or deep purple leaves. They thrive in most soils, survive drought and cold winters, and will even tolerate fairly deep shade. Simply cut back long or wayward stems in summer after flowering.

***Weigela* 'Eva Rathke'** is a tall variety with bright pink flowers set against dark green leaves.

## DUTCH GARLIC *ALLIUM HOLLANDICUM*

**HEIGHT AND SPREAD** 36 × 10 in (90 × 25 cm)
**SOIL** Well drained
**HARDINESS** Fully hardy
**SUN** ☼ ◑

Planting Dutch garlic bulbs through the middle of your border in the fall will add color and drama the following spring, when they will produce lance-shaped leaves that fade as their tall stems of purple pompom flowers appear. These bulbs thrive in well-drained soil, and are best planted among other perennials to help disguise their fading foliage. Sculptural seed heads follow the flowers and last until midsummer. Once planted, alliums pop up annually; note their positions to avoid digging up the dormant bulbs in error.

**'Purple Sensation'** is one of the best spring-flowering alliums, with pompom purple flowers.

## MASTERWORT *ASTRANTIA MAJOR*

**HEIGHT AND SPREAD** 24 × 20 in (60 × 50 cm)
**SOIL** Moist but well drained
**HARDINESS** Fully hardy
**SUN** ☼ ◑

Masterwort is a great filler plant for a low-maintenance garden, its whitish-green, pink or dark red flowers appearing in summer over decorative lobed leaves. From a distance, the blooms look unassuming, but a closer inspection reveals an intricate beauty, so plant it where you can enjoy these details. A tough perennial plant that thrives in part shade, rarely needs watering during dry spells, and will tolerate anything winter throws at it, masterwort appears each spring and spreads gradually to form a good-size clump.

**Astrantias** come in shades of pink, dark red, or whitish-green and will grow well in shady areas.

## CUSICK'S CAMASS *CAMASSIA CUSICKII*

**HEIGHT AND SPREAD** 24 × 4 in (60 × 10 cm)
**SOIL** Moist but well drained
**HARDINESS** Fully hardy
**SUN** ☼ ◑

Not as well known as it deserves, Cusick's camass is an elegant bulb used to inject late spring color, when its spikes of star-shaped, purple-blue flowers appear. Plant the bulbs in the fall in well-drained soil and the plants will reveal themselves the following year. The flowers last just a few weeks, so add other perennials in front to disguise the stems as they die down and become dormant over summer. Drought-tolerant and hardy, these beautiful bulbs require no attention after the initial planting.

**Plant bulbs** of Cusick's camass in the fall to enjoy their tall flower spikes the next spring.

## MONTBRETIA *CROCOSMIA*

**HEIGHT AND SPREAD** up to 36 × 24 in (90 × 60 cm)
**SOIL** Moist but well drained
**HARDINESS** Hardy to 14°F (−10°C)
**SUN** ☼ ◑

For a reliable plant that flowers in a range of fiery colors from late summer to early fall, look no further than montbretia. The tall, strappy foliage of this perennial contrasts with the sparkling orange, red, or yellow blooms, which open over a few weeks and lift borders that may look tired at this time of year. It is not a plant for a very cold garden, but given a sheltered spot and well-drained soil, it will produce a trouble-free clump. If plants become too large, dig out a section in spring as the new shoots appear.

**Montbretia's fiery flowers** provide much-needed color as summer fades into fall.

## HARDY GERANIUM *GERANIUM*

**HEIGHT AND SPREAD** up to 36 × 24 in (90 × 60 cm)
**SOIL** Any, except very wet
**HARDINESS** Fully hardy
**SUN** ☼ ◐ ☀

Most hardy geraniums, or cranesbills, are very adaptable, easy-care perennials. They are ideal for filling gaps in borders with their clumps of divided leaves and saucer-shaped flowers. Some, such as *Geranium sanguineum*, prefer full sun, while *G. phaeum* is happy in shade; others prefer a few hours of shade during the day. They grow well in most garden soils. One of the best is ROZANNE, which flowers nonstop from late spring to fall, its white-centered blue flowers almost obscuring the marbled, lobed foliage.

**ROZANNE** is a free-flowering geranium that produces blue flowers from spring to fall.

## AVENS *GEUM*

**HEIGHT AND SPREAD** up to 20 × 12 in (50 × 30 cm)
**SOIL** Moist but well drained
**HARDINESS** Fully hardy
**SUN** ☼ ◐

Providing splashes of bright color from early summer to midsummer, avens forms rosettes of scalloped leaves below saucer-shaped red, orange, yellow, or pink flowers held on wiry stems. This compact perennial is very easy to grow and will thrive in most gardens with little attention, once established. You can remove the old flowering stems to encourage new blooms to form, or do nothing and accept a slightly shorter season of color. Divide clumps in spring or fall if they spread beyond their allocated area.

*Geum* **'Borisii'** is ideal for the front of a border, where its fiery orange flowers can shine.

## FALL SEDUM *HYLOTELEPHIUM SPECTABILE*

**HEIGHT AND SPREAD** up to 24 × 24 in (60 × 60 cm)
**SOIL** Well drained
**HARDINESS** Fully hardy
**SUN** ☼

The ice plant, sometimes listed under its former name *Sedum spectabile*, produces sturdy stems of gray-green, fleshy foliage that emerges before the flat heads of starry pink or white flowers appear in late summer. Use the leafy stems to create a colorful edge to the front of a border and plant spring and early summer flowers behind them. Tolerant of drought and even a little shade, this plant is very easy to grow. If, after a few years, the stems start to splay out, dig up clumps in spring and replant healthy sections.

**The flat-headed blooms** of the ice plant contribute swathes of color from late summer.

## SHASTA DAISY *LEUCANTHEMUM × SUPERBUM*

**HEIGHT AND SPREAD** up to 5 ×3 ft (1.5 × 1 m)
**SOIL** Moist but well drained
**HARDINESS** Hardy to 5°F (–15°C)
**SUN** ☼ ◐

The striking large white daisies of these summer-flowering perennials create impact in the center of a border. Most reach about 3 ft (1 m) in height, although some may grow a little taller, and shorter varieties such as 'Snowcap' are also available for small spaces. The taller forms of these classic cottage plants may need staking if grown in part shade, as their stems reach for the sun, but they are generally easy to grow and rarely need watering once well established. They spread to form clumps that can be divided in fall or spring.

**Tall and double-flowered,** 'Wirral Supreme' is perfect for the middle or back of a bed.

## SNOWFLAKE *LEUCOJUM AESTIVUM*

**HEIGHT AND SPREAD** 16 × 6 in (40 × 15 cm)
**SOIL** Moist but well drained
**HARDINESS** Fully hardy
**SUN** ☀ ◐

Snowflake is usually in flower from early spring, its slender stems adorned with large snowdrop-like blooms. Plant the bulbs in drifts through a border in the fall; strappy leaves will then appear in late winter, followed by sturdy stems bearing the white and green pendent flowers. Site them behind later-flowering perennials or small shrubs that will disguise the gap left in summer when their foliage dies down. This beautiful bulb looks after itself and appears year after year.

**'Gravetye Giant'** has large bell-shaped flowers and blooms for many weeks in spring.

## DAFFODIL *NARCISSUS*

**HEIGHT AND SPREAD** up to 16 × 6 in (40 × 15 cm)
**SOIL** Any, except wet
**HARDINESS** Fully hardy
**SUN** ☀ ◐

With thousands of varieties to choose from, daffodils can grace your borders from late winter to late spring. For an easy-care bed, choose those with smaller blooms and slim, strappy leaves, such as 'Thalia', 'Hawera', 'Jetfire', and the early-flowering 'February Gold'. Plant bulbs between later-flowering plants in the fall for blooms the following spring. They will then reappear every year if you leave the foliage to die naturally after flowering; the smaller types are less conspicuous as they fade.

**'February Gold'** is one of the earliest to flower, its bright blooms opening from late winter.

## CATMINT *NEPETA RACEMOSA*

**HEIGHT AND SPREAD** up to 24 × 36 in (60 × 90 cm)
**SOIL** Any except very wet
**HARDINESS** Fully hardy
**SUN** ☀ ◐

Despite its common name, this species rarely attracts cats (try *Nepeta* × *faassenii* if you are a cat-lover), but its small, pollen-rich, blue-mauve summer flowers will appeal to butterflies and bees. An easy-going plant, catmint will grow in almost any soil, sails through periods of drought and wet winter weather, and forms a neat mound on free-draining soils—it may sprawl on clays. 'Walker's Low' is one of the best cultivars and produces a long show of blooms if you cut off the first faded flower heads.

**Catmint** is great value, its small flowers blooming over a long period in summer.

## BORDER PHLOX *PHLOX PANICULATA*

**HEIGHT AND SPREAD** up to 4 × 3 ft (1.2 × 1 m)
**SOIL** Moist but well drained
**HARDINESS** Fully hardy
**SUN** ☀ ◐

Border phlox is an elegant perennial grown for its tall stems of small, saucer-shaped, fragrant flowers. These come in a range of colors, including purple, white, pink, and red. Happy in some shade and most garden soils, except for very free-draining, it is easy to care for. If you want to avoid staking the stems, plant it in a sheltered position to protect it from high winds, or choose a short variety such as 'Roberta' or 'Alexandra' and plant it in the middle of a border, where other plants will offer some protection.

**Large heads** of fragrant, lilac blooms make 'Franz Schubert' a good choice for a sheltered site.

## BLACK-EYED SUSAN *RUDBECKIA FULGIDA*

**HEIGHT AND SPREAD** up to 32 × 20 in (80 × 50 cm)
**SOIL** Moist but well drained
**HARDINESS** Fully hardy
**SUN** ☼ ☼

The sunny golden daisies of black-eyed susans, or coneflowers as they are also known, shine out from a border when they appear from late summer to early fall. *R. fulgida* var. *sullivantii* 'Goldsturm' and *R. fulgida* var. *deamii* are both compact forms and their sturdy stems will not need staking. These plants are happy on heavier clays or soils that do not dry out quickly in summer, although they will recover from short periods of drought. Plant them toward the front of a sunny border for the best display of flowers.

*Rudbeckia fulgida* **var. deamii** produces stout stems of bright yellow flowers in late summer.

## BALKAN CLARY *SALVIA NEMOROSA*

**HEIGHT AND SPREAD** up to 20 × 12 in (50 × 30 cm)
**SOIL** Moist but well drained
**HARDINESS** Fully hardy
**SUN** ☼

Unlike bedding salvias that last just one season, these tough perennial plants will reappear each year, their spikes of purple flowers lasting for many weeks from summer to early fall. Plant them in groups toward the front of a sunny border for the best results—they will tolerate a few hours of shade each day, as long as they receive midday sun. If you want an even longer season of blooms, cut faded stems back to stimulate new growth. Drought-tolerant once established, these decorative plants rarely need watering.

**Plant Balkan clary** for its purple flower spikes loved by bees and butterflies.

## LAMB'S EAR *STACHYS BYZANTINA*

**HEIGHT AND SPREAD** up to 8 × 18 in (20 × 45 cm)
**SOIL** Well drained
**HARDINESS** Fully hardy
**SUN** ☼

Grown primarily for its velvety silver foliage, this carpeting evergreen perennial makes a great weed-suppressing mat at the front of a sunny border. The spikes of small purple or pink flowers attract bees and other pollinating insects when they appear in summer. If grown in free-draining soil (it dislikes wet conditions), this easy-care plant rarely requires watering once it's established. Try lamb's ear in a gravel garden or the edge of a raised bed, too. If you only want leaf interest, opt for 'Silver Carpet', which rarely flowers.

**The velvety foliage** of lamb's ear cries out to be touched when planted within easy reach.

## CULVER'S ROOT *VERONICASTRUM VIRGINICUM*

**HEIGHT AND SPREAD** up to 6 ft × 20 in (1.8 m × 50 cm)
**SOIL** Any, except wet
**HARDINESS** Fully hardy
**SUN** ☼ ☼

A tall perennial ideal for the back of a border, culver's root produces sturdy stems of small green leaves and spikes of tiny light violet-blue or white flowers in summer and early fall. The blooms are also rich in pollen and attract bees. It is best grown on clay soils that retain moisture in summer and rarely needs staking, unless it is in a windy spot. It also copes well with low winter temperatures. Plant spring and early summer flowers in front of it, so the leafy stems can provide a textured foil for the blooms.

**Culver's root's** tall flower spikes make a striking statement at the back of a border.

# EASY-CARE RAISED BEDS

Raised beds are easy to make from scratch or flat-packs and can offer you a growing space where there is no soil, such as on a patio. Like a container, they will need drainage at the bottom, so bear this in mind when creating one on a hard surface. Visually, they make beautiful design features, adding height and color to the space, while also offering ideal growing conditions for many flowers, herbs, and crops.

**Raised beds** of about hip height are easy to tend and create a dramatic statement.

## RAISING YOUR GAME

There are some good reasons for installing a raised bed or two, especially if you want to grow plants that do not suit your soil type. For example, if you love rhododendrons and camellias, which need acid conditions to thrive, but your soil is alkaline (see *p.12*), you can fill a raised bed with acidic growing mix and feed the plants with fertilizer for acid-loving plants to keep them happy.

In a shady yard, raising the growing space can allow more sunlight to reach the plants, widening your choices. And if you garden on heavy clay soil that is prone to waterlogging, the free-draining conditions in a raised bed will instantly alleviate the problem. Plants at knee- or hip-height are also easier to tend, so a raised bed would be a good choice if you have mobility issues.

Raised beds can also enhance the decorative value of your yard, creating a change in level in a flat space, and introducing new materials. You can also include trailing plants around the sides to create a veil of flowers and foliage.

**Elevating your growing space** by a notch or two can offer plants more sunlight in a shady spot.

## CHOOSING A BED

There are many flat-pack raised bed kits on the market, made from timber, recycled plastic, or other synthetic materials, which you simply screw together. When buying timber products, make sure they have the FSC (Forest Stewardship Council) logo, which shows that the wood was sourced from a sustainably managed forest, and avoid plastic that is not made from recycled materials to lower your carbon footprint.

The other option is to build a bed from scratch using new or reclaimed bricks, crossties (check that they are not impregnated with creosote or other toxic chemicals), or stacked logs from a pruned or felled tree. You can also improvise and use whatever you have on hand to create the walls, but for a low-maintenance bed always choose durable materials that will not rot easily.

The size of your bed will also partly determine its care: smaller features will demand more watering than larger beds that hold greater volumes of soil and water. However, if it is too big you may not be able to reach your plants without treading on the soil, so opt for a maximum width of 5 ft (1.5 m). Also consider creating a wide shelf around the bed to add extra seating for guests and for you while tending your plants.

**Metal cages,** known as gabions, filled with old bricks from a house build make an intriguing and durable raised bed.

## SITING YOUR BED

You can build your raised bed almost anywhere in the yard, but remember that areas next to walls or fences may be in a rain shadow and plants will therefore need more watering. Likewise, the soil will dry out quickly if your bed is located in full sun, and all raised beds will be free-draining, so consider how you will keep your plants irrigated during dry weather. You can either install an automatic watering system for easy maintenance (see pp.130–131) or, if your plants are suitable, site the bed in a shadier place where evaporation rates will be lower.

When installing a bed on a paved patio or courtyard, remember that the necessary drainage means that dirty water will seep out from under it and could stain your floor. To avoid this, if possible, take up some of the paving or concrete so that water can drain directly into the soil beneath your bed.

**Filled with ferns** and barrenwort, this raised bed located in shade will rarely need watering in the cool conditions.

**Patio roses** and perennial flowering plants are easy to grow in a brick bed.

## WHAT TO GROW

Most plants will thrive in a raised bed, although thirsty species, such as globe flowers (*Trollius*) and arum lilies (*Zantedeschia*), would not be happy in the free-draining conditions. Planting a tree may not be advisable in a small space, since the added height could create more shade where it is not needed. Check the final sizes of shrubs, as some might take over the entire bed within a few years.

Herbs; most perennial and annual flowers, especially those that can cope with drought; and crops such as salad leaves, beets, and strawberries, would be great choices for a raised bed.

**TOP TIP** UNLESS YOU ARE INCLUDING ACID-LOVING PLANTS, THE BEST ACIDIC GROWING MEDIUM FOR A RAISED BED IS A 3:2:7 MIX OF WELL-ROTTED MANURE OR COMPOST, SHARP SAND, AND TOPSOIL.

# RAISED-BED ORNAMENTALS

Like giant containers, raised beds can offer fussy plants the specific soil conditions they require, while providing enough space for the roots of larger species to expand. The selection here includes trailers to edge a bed, "fillers" to create an impact in the center, and plants that may not be suitable for your soil. All are easy to care for and require little attention apart from watering in hot or windy weather. You can also mix and match them with herbs (*see pp.68–69*) and other seasonal flowers recommended for containers (*see pp.80–89*).

## DYER'S CHAMOMILE *ANTHEMIS TINCTORIA*

**HEIGHT AND SPREAD** up to 32 × 32 in (80 × 80 cm)
**GROWING MEDIUM** Peat-free with added sand
**HARDINESS** Fully hardy
**SUN** ☼

The long-lasting yellow or white daisy flowers of dyer's chamomile appear over ferny aromatic foliage, creating a lively display throughout summer. This clump-forming perennial thrives in the free-draining soil of a raised bed, but choose a compact variety or put a plant support ring over the emerging stems of taller types to prevent them flopping. Cut the faded flower stems back to the base to encourage new growth to form. Each plant may live for just a few years, but dyer's chamomile often self-seeds.

**The tall stems of 'E. C. Buxton'** lend height to the center of a raised-bed display.

## NODDING ONION *ALLIUM CERNUUM*

**HEIGHT AND SPREAD** 18 × 6 in (45 × 15 cm)
**GROWING MEDIUM** Peat-free
**HARDINESS** Fully hardy
**SUN** ☼

Most alliums enjoy the free-draining conditions in a raised bed but nodding onion is a particularly good choice, allowing you to view the dainty chandeliers of small, bell-shaped summer flowers at close range. The narrow, strap-shaped leaves appear first in spring and die down before the flowering stems emerge. Plant the bulbs in the fall for a display the following year; they will then reappear each summer thereafter. Clumps usually increase year-on-year if you remove the seed heads.

**Growing nodding onion** in a raised bed allows you to view the dainty flowers up close.

## WORMWOOD *ARTEMISIA*

**HEIGHT AND SPREAD** up to 30 × 24 in (75 × 60 cm)
**GROWING MEDIUM** Peat-free with added sand
**HARDINESS** Hardy to 5°F (−15°C)
**SUN** ☼

Traditionally used as an herbal remedy to ease digestive complaints, wormwood is also a beautiful plant, grown for its aromatic silver foliage. Popular varieties include the lacy-leaved 'Powys Castle' and the larger *Artemisia ludoviciana* 'Silver Queen', with its broader grayish-white foliage. These perennials are semi-evergreen and may lose a few leaves in cold winters. Add some sand to the soil to keep them happy, and trim the stems down to healthy buds in spring to promote bushier growth.

***Artemisia ludoviciana* 'Silver Queen'** produces a mound of bright silver foliage.

## AUBRIETA *AUBRIETA*

**HEIGHT AND SPREAD** 4 × 12 in (10 × 30 cm)
**GROWING MEDIUM** Peat-free
**HARDINESS** Fully hardy
**SUN** ☼ ☀

Aubrieta is a trailing evergreen perennial that will soften the edge of a raised bed with its small green leaves and tiny spring flowers, available in shades of pink, purple, and white. You can also buy variegated forms, such as 'Argenteovariegata', with cream-edged foliage. Almost maintenance-free, aubrieta will flower annually if you do nothing at all, but it may bloom again in the summer if the stems are cut back just after the first flush has faded. Rejuvenate old plants by pruning in late spring.

**Aubrieta's** trailing stems of gray-green leaves and colorful spring flowers make a beautiful edging plant for a raised bed.

## TRAILING BELLFLOWER *CAMPANULA POSCHARSKYANA*

**HEIGHT AND SPREAD** 8 × 24 in (20 × 60 cm)
**GROWING MEDIUM** Peat-free
**HARDINESS** Hardy to 5°F (−15°C)
**SUN** ☼ ☀

The trailing bellflower is one of the easiest campanulas to grow, rarely succumbing to pests and diseases and delivering a colorful cascade of flowering stems throughout summer. The small, starry blooms appear over rounded, deciduous leaves and come in blue, lilac, or pink. The blue species is the most vigorous, so choose another color if you have limited space for it in your bed. This little plant is very undemanding and can be left to its own devices—just cut back unwanted stems in spring to keep it in check.

**'Lisduggan Variety'** creates a curtain of trailing, leafy stems and lilac flowers in summer.

## RED VALERIAN *CENTRANTHUS RUBER*

**HEIGHT AND SPREAD** 32 × 18 in (80 × 45 cm)
**GROWING MEDIUM** Peat-free
**HARDINESS** Hardy to 5°F (−15°C)
**SUN** ☼ ☀

Almost infallible when grown in full sun and free-draining soil, red valerian will provide plenty of summer color in a raised bed. Heads of tiny, slightly fragrant flowers, which are available in crimson, pink, or white, bloom continuously from late spring to fall over gray-green foliage. Despite the long floral show, this perennial requires almost no maintenance—just remove faded stems in the fall or spring to make way for new growth, or snip off the flowers as soon as they fade to prevent them self-seeding.

**Red valerian** will brighten up a raised bed in summer with its clusters of small pink blooms.

## CLEMATIS *CLEMATIS* (COMPACT CULTIVARS)

**HEIGHT AND SPREAD** 4 × 4 ft (1.2 × 1.2 m)
**GROWING MEDIUM** Peat-free
**HARDINESS** Fully hardy
**SUN** ☼

Use this deciduous climber to create a beautiful centerpiece in a raised bed, or train the twining stems to cover a wired wall or fence (see p.51) directly behind it. Among the best compact types are the Evipo range by Raymond Evison, which bloom all summer. Plant the crown (where the roots meet the stems) 2 in (5 cm) below the surface of the soil and provide a support such as a cane pyramid or slim-gauged trellis for the stems to climb. To prune, reduce all stems down to 6 in (15 cm) in late winter.

**Ooh La La** is a compact variety that will grow well in a raised bed or large pot.

## MAGELLAN RYE GRASS *ELYMUS MAGELLANICUS*

**HEIGHT AND SPREAD** 24 × 24 in (60 × 60 cm)
**GROWING MEDIUM** Topsoil
**HARDINESS** Fully hardy
**SUN** ☼

Grown for its sparkling bright blue leaves, this clump-forming grass is a great asset to a raised bed display. The buff-colored flower spikes, which appear in summer, add to its charms. It is semi-evergreen and may lose some or all of its leaves in a harsh winter, but new growth will appear in spring. Your only task is to thread your fingers through the foliage in spring and pull out any dead growth. The smaller grass *Festuca glauca* also sports blue leaves but it is shorter-lived.

**The steely blue leaves** of this rye grass combine well with pastel or hot-hued flowers.

## CLIFF-DWELLING STONECROP

### *HYLOTELEPHIUM CAUTICOLA*

**HEIGHT AND SPREAD** 8 × 16 in (20 × 40 cm)
**GROWING MEDIUM** Peat-free with added sand
**HARDINESS** Hardy to 5°F (−15°C)
**SUN** ☼ ☼

The stems of the cliff-dwelling stonecrop trail equally well from a raised bed as they do from rocky outcrops in its native Japan. This perennial's fleshy pink-tinged, bluish-green leaves offer color from early spring, while the starry purplish-pink flowers create a late-season finale in the fall, providing a feast for pollinators. Grow it in full sun, or a little light shade, and remove the old flowering stems in early spring.

**'Lidakense'** has purple-flushed, blue-green leaves and star-shaped, rose-pink flowers in early fall.

## BULBOUS IRIS *IRIS*

**HEIGHT AND SPREAD** up to 24 × 8 in (60 × 20 cm)
**GROWING MEDIUM** Peat-free with added sand
**HARDINESS** Fully hardy
**SUN** ☼

Irises can grow from corms or bulbs, and the latter are ideal for a raised bed. The dwarf, early spring-flowering *Iris reticulata* is a good choice and produces small, spidery flowers in a range of colors, from blue and purple to yellow and white. Plant the bulbs in the fall for a display the following year—the flowers will appear for a few years but more bulbs may then need to be planted. The taller Dutch iris (*Iris hollandica*) is planted in the same way, but won't need sand, preferring damper soil.

**'Clairette'** is a little reticulata iris with grassy leaves and small, blue, early spring flowers.

## BLACK LILYTURF *OPHIOPOGON PLANISCAPUS* 'KOKURYU'

**HEIGHT AND SPREAD** 8 × 12 in (20 × 30 cm)
**GROWING MEDIUM** Peat-free
**HARDINESS** Fully hardy
**SUN** ☼ ☼

Also sold as *Ophiopogon planiscapus* 'Nigrescens', black lilyturf creates a clump of shiny black, grassy foliage that will flow gracefully over the edge of a raised bed. Short spikes of small mauve flowers appear in summer, followed by purplish-black berries. Lilyturf rarely suffers attacks from pests and diseases and thrives in sun or a little shade. It is also practically maintenance-free, and you only need to remove old foliage in spring to keep it neat. Plants will grow into a sizable clump over time.

**Black lilyturf** makes a good match for colorful grasses and small species tulips.

## CREEPING PHLOX *PHLOX SUBULATA*

**HEIGHT AND SPREAD** 6 × 12 in (15 × 30 cm)
**GROWING MEDIUM** Peat-free
**HARDINESS** Fully hardy
**SUN** ☼ ◐

Not to be confused with the taller border phlox, this low-growing evergreen or semi-evergreen perennial forms a dense mat of leafy stems that will trail slightly to soften the edge of a raised bed. In summer, it bears a profusion of rounded or star-shaped flowers in shades of white, red, pink, purple, and blue, often with contrasting central eyes. Best for full sun, it will also grow in dappled shade. To maintain it, simply clip back straggly stems after flowering to encourage bushy growth.

**'Lilacina'** is a sought-after variety with slightly trailing stems of pearly lilac flowers.

## PIERIS *PIERIS*

**HEIGHT AND SPREAD** up to 6 × 6 ft (2 × 2 m)
**GROWING MEDIUM** Slightly acidic
**HARDINESS** Hardy to 5°F (−15°C)
**SUN** ☼ ◐

The most popular forms of this acid-loving evergreen shrub are *P. japonica* and its cultivars, many of which are ideally suited to a raised bed filled with an acidic medium. Choose a dwarf cultivar such as 'Ralto' or 'Katsura' as others may outgrow their space. Pieris is also known as the lily-of-the-valley shrub, due to its similar bell-shaped spring flowers in shades of white, pink, or red. Little pruning is needed; just remove unwanted growth or crossing stems in late winter.

**'Katsura'** is a compact cultivar with pale pink flowers, followed by the new foliage, which emerges deep red before turning green.

## DWARF RHODODENDRON *RHODODENDRON*

**HEIGHT AND SPREAD** up to 4 × 4 ft (1.2 × 1.2 m)
**GROWING MEDIUM** Slightly acidic
**HARDINESS** Fully hardy
**SUN** ☼

While many rhododendrons are large shrubs that would soon outgrow a raised bed, dwarf varieties that reach 3 ft (1 m) or less in height and spread are ideal candidates. Their glossy evergreen leaves provide year-round color, and in spring, large funnel-shaped pink, red, purple, or white flowers produce a spectacular display. Plant them in a sheltered, partly shaded bed filled with an acidic medium. Apply a feed for acid-loving shrubs each spring and prune lightly after flowering if need be.

**'Wee Bee'** is a dwarf evergreen rhododendron with frilly-edged, rose-pink flowers.

## SPECIES TULIPS *TULIPA*

**HEIGHT AND SPREAD** up to 12 × 6 in (30 × 15 cm)
**GROWING MEDIUM** Peat-free with added sand
**HARDINESS** Fully hardy
**SUN** ☼

Unlike the large-flowered border tulips, these small, daintier species flower reliably each year with no maintenance. Usually listed as "botanical or species miniature tulips," they bear strappy leaves and small cup- or slim vase-shaped flowers in shades of white, pink, red, orange, and yellow. Plant the bulbs in the fall at the front of a bed where you can admire the spring blooms, and mark their position so you don't dig them up when the foliage dies down in summer.

**'Peppermintstick'** is a hybrid of *Tulipa clusiana* with pink-striped white flowers.

# MAKING A MICRO WOODLAND

**Trees bring many benefits to the yard, including height and structure, colorful blossom, food for pollinators, and nesting sites for birds, to name just a few. A tree that's suited to your conditions and the space you have available can be very easy to care for, once established, while a layer of woodland plants beneath it will reduce weed growth. The best time to plant a tree is in late fall or early spring.**

**Multi-stemmed trees** are a good choice for small spaces as they tend not to grow as tall as those with a single stem.

**Dwarf fruit trees** are ideal for small urban spaces, growing to just 6½ft (2 m) or less in height and spread.

## CHOOSING THE RIGHT TREE

The key to creating an easy-care mini woodland is to check that the tree you plant will be happy in your yard (see pp.12–13). Look on tree nursery websites and make a list of those you like, then compare their needs to the conditions your yard offers, such as hours of sun or shade, soil type, and the space available. A tree that won't outgrow its allotted position will need little if any pruning, and if it likes your site and soil it will grow well with almost no help from you once its roots are well established.

## WHERE TO PLANT

Finding the right spot for a tree will ensure that it does not outgrow its space or cast too much shade, which in turn will keep pruning to a minimum. You can use a tree to shade a patio in summer, but check that it won't plunge it into darkness all year, which won't be such a boon—you can monitor this by placing a ladder where you plan to site it. Also plant at least 12–15 ft (4–5 m) from the house if your tree will grow to 10 ft (3 m) in height, or further away for a larger specimen, and avoid sites close to boundary fences and walls, where the soil will be drier and the tree may cast shade over your neighbor's property.

**Plant trees** in areas where they will not cast shade in neighboring yards.

**Shade-loving geraniums** and ferns are ideally suited to a site beneath a hawthorn tree (*Crataegus*).

## PLANTING FILLS

Many beautiful shrubs, ferns, bulbs, and other flowering plants grow naturally in woodlands and can be used to decorate the area beneath your trees, while minimizing the space available for weeds to take hold. Choose from the easy-care options on pp.46–49, which need little aftercare once established, although they will require regular watering initially. Plant them at least 3 ft (1 m) from the tree trunk.

# PLANTING A POTTED TREE

1 Leave the tree in its pot in a bucket of water for about an hour to soak the root ball. Dig a square hole three times as wide and the same depth as the pot. Use a fork to loosen the soil around the sides.

2 Place the tree in the hole and, using a cane laid across the top, check that the point where the roots meet the stem will be level with, or slightly above, the soil surface.

3 Remove the tree from its pot and, with your fingers, gently loosen any roots coiled around the side of the root ball. Place it in the hole. Fill in around the root ball with soil and use your toe to gently press it down to remove any large air pockets.

4 Large trees will also need staking. Hammer in a sturdy wooden stake at a 45° angle on the side of the tree opposite to the prevailing wind direction. Attach it with a tree tie.

5 Water the tree well and then add a 2 in (5 cm) layer of well-rotted manure or garden compost, or aged chipped bark (see p.128), over the root area, leaving a gap around the trunk.

6 Trees need watering regularly during dry spells for three years after planting to ensure the roots establish well. To make this task easier, install a drip or seep hose (see p.131) over the root area and attach it to a timer on an outside tap when dry, warmer weather arrives. Set the timer for an hour once or twice a week—just check that the soil does not become waterlogged and reduce the watering frequency if this problem arises. Thereafter, the tree will not need watering unless extreme drought conditions persist over many months.

**TOP TIP** EACH SPRING AFTER IT HAS RAINED, RENEW THE MULCH AROUND YOUR TREE TO TRAP MOISTURE IN THE SOIL AND SLOWLY FEED THE ROOTS.

# WOODLAND PLANTS

Choose from this selection of small to medium-size trees to create height and a sculptural feature in your yard that offers year-round interest. Even the bare branches of a deciduous tree in winter can create a beautiful focal point, animated by birds using them as look-outs. With a layer of easy-care foliage and flowering plants beneath the canopies to help suppress weeds, you can create a tiny woodland environment that offers food for pollinators and a sanctuary for wildlife, but requires little work from you once all the plants are well-established.

## PAPERBARK MAPLE *ACER GRISEUM*

**HEIGHT AND SPREAD** 25 × 12 ft (8 × 4 m)
**SOIL** Any, except wet
**HARDINESS** Hardy to 5°C (−15°C)
**SUN** ☼ ☼

This graceful deciduous tree has many points of interest, including its cinnamon-colored, peeling bark, which becomes most noticeable in winter when its silhouette of bare stems is revealed. Small green spring flowers develop into winged seed heads in the fall, when the green divided leaves fire up into dazzling shades of red and orange, delivering a spectacular finale to the season. This compact tree does not need pruning, apart from the removal of dead or damaged stems in summer or late fall.

**The peeling bark** of this elegant maple creates a textural focal point in a small space.

## JAPANESE MAPLE *ACER PALMATUM*

**HEIGHT AND SPREAD** 12 × 12 ft (4 × 4 m)
**SOIL** Moist but well drained
**HARDINESS** Fully hardy
**SUN** ☼

Loved for their luminous displays of red, orange, or yellow fall foliage, in spring Japanese maples also produce small red flowers, followed by winged red or green seed heads. Avoid varieties with finely dissected foliage, which is prone to drying out in summer; good choices for a low-maintenance yard are 'Atropurpureum', 'Osakazuki', and 'Fireglow'. All need some shade, especially at midday, and a site out of strong winds, but are otherwise easy to care for and need no regular pruning.

**'Osakazuki',** with its bright fall color, is a good choice for an easy-care yard.

## SERVICEBERRY *AMELANCHIER GRANDIFLORA*

**HEIGHT AND SPREAD** 12 × 12 ft (4 × 4 m)
**SOIL** Any, except very alkaline
**HARDINESS** Fully hardy
**SUN** ☼ ☼

Also known as Juneberry, due to its small, red or dark purple summer fruits, the serviceberry is a stalwart of the small, easy-care yard. As the bronze-tinged foliage unfurls in spring, clusters of small white flowers appear, tinged pink in some varieties. The leaves turn dark green in summer before putting on a bright reddish-purple guise in the fall. Tolerant of sun or part shade, this compact little tree requires no regular pruning. Just check your soil pH as it will not thrive in very alkaline conditions (see p.12).

**Serviceberry** produces white spring flowers that stand out from bronze-tinged young leaves.

## HIMALAYAN BIRCH *BETULA UTILIS* VAR. *JACQUEMONTII*

**HEIGHT AND SPREAD** up to 25 ×12 ft (8 × 4 m)
**SOIL** Any, except wet
**HARDINESS** Fully hardy
**SUN** ☼ ☼

Grown primarily for its white bark, the Himalayan birch lends a naturalistic woodland look to an easy-care yard. This elegant deciduous tree sports yellowy-brown catkins in spring and dark green leaves that turn buttery-yellow in the fall. However, it really comes into its own in winter when its network of bare branches creates a ghostly outline against the sky or dark evergreen shrubs. Happy in full sun or light dappled shade, it is tolerant of most soils and will not need regular pruning to retain its pyramidal shape.

**The bark** of the Himalayan birch peels each year to reveal clean white stems beneath.

## JUDAS TREE *CERCIS SILIQUASTRUM*

**HEIGHT AND SPREAD** 12 × 12 ft (4 × 4 m)
**SOIL** Well drained
**HARDINESS** Hardy to 5°C (−15°C)
**SUN** ☼ ☼

This small deciduous tree is ideal for sheltered areas. In spring, it lights up the yard with deep pink flowers held on bare stems, and bright green, heart-shaped leaves that unfurl soon afterward. Reddish-purple flattened seed heads appear in the fall, hanging from the branches like tassels alongside the yellow foliage. Few small trees offer such great value while requiring so little care. Its compact size means that pruning is rarely required, and it will tolerate most soils, except wet clays.

**The Judas tree** is ideal for a small space, where it will offer color from spring to fall.

## HAWTHORN *CRATAEGUS LAEVIGATA*

**HEIGHT AND SPREAD** 15 × 12 ft (5 × 4 m)
**SOIL** Any, except wet
**HARDINESS** Fully hardy
**SUN** ☼ ☼

Hawthorn is a tough little deciduous tree, tolerant of all climates and most soils, making it ideal for any low-maintenance yard. It has its charms, too, with lobed leaves and thorny stems, which in late spring are decorated with large clusters of small white or pink flowers, loved by bees. In the fall, red berries appear, and persist until they are eaten by birds. Even in winter, the gnarled stems of a mature tree create a decorative feature. It needs no pruning, but wayward stems can be removed in late fall or early winter.

**'Rosea Flore Pleno'** is a beautiful form, with pink double flowers in spring.

## HONEY LOCUST *GLEDITSIA TRIACANTHOS*

**HEIGHT AND SPREAD** 15 × 10 ft (5 × 3 m)
**SOIL** Any, except wet
**HARDINESS** Fully hardy
**SUN** ☼

The most widely available honey locust is the golden-leaved *Gleditsia triacanthos* f. *inermis* 'Sunburst', which makes a dramatic focal point in spring as the foliage unfurls. The divided leaves then mellow to lime-green but turn bright yellow again in the fall before dropping. The large, flattened seedpods also appear at this time, having developed from inconspicuous spring flowers. Reasonably compact, the honey locust does not require regular pruning. Plant it in full sun for the brightest foliage colors.

**The bright yellow leaves** of 'Sunburst' create a mesmerizing focal point in spring.

## HOLLY *ILEX*

**HEIGHT AND SPREAD** up to 20 × 12 ft (6 × 4 m)
**SOIL** Any, except wet
**HARDINESS** Fully hardy
**SUN** ☼ ◐

Hollies are generally compact, upright trees, perfect for small spaces where their foliage provides year-round color. Choose a cultivar of the English holly (*Ilex aquifolium*) or the Highclere holly (*I. × altaclerensis*), which tends to be less prickly. Both come in a range of sizes, so look for one that suits your location, and choose a female plant if you want the red berries. Hollies tolerate most soils and do not require regular pruning. Remove lower branches in spring for a more treelike appearance.

**Ilex × altaclerensis 'Lawsoniana'** is an almost spineless holly that produces bright red berries in the fall.

## CRAB APPLE *MALUS*

**HEIGHT AND SPREAD** up to 25 × 12 ft (8 × 4 m)
**SOIL** Any, except wet
**HARDINESS** Fully hardy
**SUN** ☼ ◐

Crab apples are deservedly popular, bearing profuse pink or white spring blossom, followed in the fall by small, bitter-tasting apples, some of which can be used to make jam. These deciduous small to medium-size trees are tolerant of pollution, fully hardy, and not fussy about soil type. Among the best cultivars are 'John Downie', with its large fruits, ideal for culinary use; 'Evereste', which produces masses of orange- or yellow-tinged red crab apples; and the golden-fruited 'Butterball'.

**'John Downie'** is a beautiful feature tree that produces colorful fruits in the fall.

## FLOWERING CHERRY *PRUNUS*

**HEIGHT AND SPREAD** up to 20 × 12 ft (6 × 4 m)
**SOIL** Any, except wet
**HARDINESS** Fully hardy
**SUN** ☼

Most flowering cherries are compact, deciduous trees suitable for small spaces, but do check before buying as some grow larger. They are grown mainly for their pink or white spring blossom, but some, such as P. 'Kanzan', P. × incam 'Okamé', and P. 'Pink Perfection', also put on a show in the fall when their foliage turns orange and red. Flowering cherries tolerate low winter temperatures and are happy in most soils. Pruning is not needed, but you can remove misplaced branches in summer.

**Prunus × incam 'Okamé'** offers pink blossom and red and orange fall leaves.

## BLACK CHERRY PLUM *PRUNUS CERASIFERA*

**HEIGHT AND SPREAD** up to 25 × 12 ft (8 × 4 m)
**SOIL** Any, except wet
**HARDINESS** Fully hardy
**SUN** ☼

A small to medium-size deciduous tree with huge impact, the black cherry plum features almost black stems which in spring are dotted with clusters of single pink flowers, loved by bees. The blooms contrast with the emerging bronze leaves that turn deep purple as the season progresses, before they take on shades of orange and red in the fall. This pretty plum will thrive in an urban space and most soils, and requires almost no maintenance—you can remove any unwanted stems in summer if need be.

**The cultivar 'Nigra'** is a good choice for its dark purple foliage and pink spring blossom.

## TIBETAN CHERRY *PRUNUS SERRULA*

**HEIGHT AND SPREAD** 20 × 12 ft (6 × 4 m)
**SOIL** Any, except wet
**HARDINESS** Fully hardy
**SUN** ☼

The main reason for growing this small to medium-size deciduous tree is its shiny, mahogany-colored bark, which peels to reveal paler tones beneath. Dazzling in winter when the stems are bare, this beautiful tree has yellow foliage in the fall and white spring flowers, followed by small, inedible red fruits. Unfussed about soil type, it will grow well even in exposed sites, but needs full sun to thrive. It does not require regular pruning; unwanted stems can be removed in summer.

**Multi-stemmed** Tibetan cherries create a colorful focal point in a winter garden.

## WILLOW-LEAVED PEAR *PYRUS SALICIFOLIA* 'PENDULA'

**HEIGHT AND SPREAD** up to 20 × 15 ft (6 × 5 m)
**SOIL** Any, except wet
**HARDINESS** Fully hardy
**SUN** ☼

This compact, weeping, deciduous tree is very undemanding. In spring, it produces arching stems of narrow, silvery-gray leaves that light up the yard. The foliage gradually darkens to gray-green during summer before turning bright yellow in the fall. Creamy-white flowers adorn the branches in spring, just as the new foliage emerges, and are followed by small, inedible fruits. In winter, remove the lower stems to leave a clear trunk so that the foliage does not trail on the ground.

**'Pendula'** is a graceful tree ideal for a small plot, with silvery leaves and white blossom.

## VILMORIN'S ROWAN *SORBUS VILMORINII*

**HEIGHT AND SPREAD** 15 × 12 ft (5 × 4 m)
**SOIL** Well drained
**HARDINESS** Fully hardy
**SUN** ☼ ☼

Many species of rowan (*Sorbus*) are good choices for small spaces, but one of the best is *S. vilmorinii*, with its compact habit and elegant, fernlike green leaves, which turn purple in the fall before falling. In spring, the stems are adorned with flat heads of creamy-white flowers, followed in the fall by pink fruits that fade to white. Easy to care for, this rowan thrives in any well-drained soil, especially if it is slightly acidic. It needs no pruning, although misplaced stems can be removed in winter.

**Vilmorin's rowan,** with its white blossom and pink berries, offers many months of interest.

## CHINESE STEWARTIA *STEWARTIA SINENSIS*

**HEIGHT AND SPREAD** up to 20 × 12 ft (6 × 4 m)
**SOIL** Moist but well drained
**HARDINESS** Hardy to 5°C (−15°C)
**SUN** ☼ ☼

Chinese stewartia is a small deciduous tree with many beautiful features, including peeling brown and purple bark that offers winter and early spring interest. In summer, large, slightly fragrant flowers decorate the stems, after which the dark green foliage turns bright crimson in the fall. Before buying, check that you can provide it with a sheltered position and soil that is not too alkaline (see *p.12*). If so, this tree will be very easy to grow, requiring no regular pruning.

**Chinese stewartia** is a medium-size tree with large, white, camellia-like flowers.

## LADY'S MANTLE *ALCHEMILLA MOLLIS*

**HEIGHT AND SPREAD** 12 x 24 in (30 x 60 cm)
**SOIL** Any
**HARDINESS** Fully hardy
**SUN** ☼ ◐

The large, scalloped, green leaves of this spreading perennial create a beautiful ruff at the edge of a woodland or shady bed. It looks most beautiful after rain, when the drops settle on the leaves. From summer to early fall, it also bears a frothy haze of tiny, lime-yellow flowers. Tolerant of most soils, including heavy clay, it is also remarkably drought-tolerant and rarely, if ever, needs watering once it is established. Just cut back old growth in spring and remove any unwanted seedlings.

**Lady's mantle** is a trouble-free perennial that produces frothy yellow summer flowers.

## JAPANESE ANEMONE *ANEMONE × HYBRIDA*

**HEIGHT AND SPREAD** up to 4 x 4 ft (1.2 x 1.2 m)
**SOIL** Any, except wet
**HARDINESS** Fully hardy
**SUN** ☼ ◐

Plant this anemone at the edge of a tree canopy, where its tall stems of round, pink or white flowers will brighten up the dappled shade. The large, lobed green leaves form a skirt beneath the blooms, which appear from late summer to early fall. This species is less vigorous than its more invasive cousin A. *hupehensis*, so take care to buy the right one if you want a well-behaved perennial that will flower year after year with no trouble. Remove the old stems in spring to make way for new growth.

**The cultivar 'Elegans'** bears pearly pink flowers during late summer and early fall.

## WOOD ANEMONE *ANEMONE NEMOROSA*

**HEIGHT AND SPREAD** 6 x 6 in (15 x 15 cm)
**SOIL** Moist but well drained
**HARDINESS** Hardy to 5°C (–15°C)
**SUN** ◐

The small, starry, white blooms of this dainty plant appear in spring over the divided green leaves, creating a carpet of flowers beneath trees and shrubs in a small woodland setting. Once you have planted the rhizomes in the fall, the plants will flower each spring, often self-seeding as the years pass. Plant in groups for the best effect. Wood anemones are not fussy about soil type, as long as it is not wet, and will tolerate drier conditions during their period of summer dormancy when the top growth dies back.

**Wood anemones** bloom underneath tree canopies just before the leaves unfurl.

## HART'S TONGUE FERN *ASPLENIUM SCOLOPENDRIUM*

**HEIGHT AND SPREAD** up to 24 x 24 in (60 x 60 cm)
**SOIL** Moist but well drained
**HARDINESS** Fully hardy
**SUN** ◐

This tough evergreen fern thrives in the dappled shade beneath a tree canopy, where it will produce a clump of wavy-edged, glossy foliage that combines well with more colorful shade-loving flowers. The cultivar 'Crispum Group' is a good choice, with crimped leaf margins that create a wonderful textural effect. It prefers part shade but will also grow in quite deep shade, and when established it tolerates dry soil conditions. The removal of dead leaves to keep it neat is all the maintenance this plant needs.

**The 'Crispum Group' fern** produces a rosette of glossy, crimped evergreen leaves.

## SPOTTED LAUREL *AUCUBA JAPONICA*

**HEIGHT AND SPREAD** up to 10 × 10 ft (3 × 3 m)
**SOIL** Any, except wet
**HARDINESS** Hardy to 5°C (−15°C)
**SUN** ☼ ☀

Grown for its green leaves with yellow spots or splashes, this evergreen shrub is invaluable for its ability to flourish in the deep shade and dry soil under a tree. It is not the most exciting plant, but provides some color where few others will thrive. Female forms such as 'Variegata' and 'Crotonifolia' also produce small purple flowers followed by bright red fall berries. It needs no attention once established, but you can cut back overly long or damaged stems in late spring after the frosts.

**For red berries** in the fall, select a female spotted laurel plant such as *Aucuba japonica* 'Variegata'.

## ELEPHANT'S EARS *BERGENIA*

**HEIGHT AND SPREAD** up to 24 × 24 in (60 × 60 cm)
**SOIL** Any, except wet
**HARDINESS** Fully hardy
**SUN** ☼ ☀

Grown for their rounded heads of small spring flowers in pink or white and large, oval leaves, often bronze- or red-tinted in winter, these evergreen perennials are ideal for the edge of a garden woodland. Most are compact plants, rarely reaching more than 20 in (50 cm) in height, and form a skirt of weed-suppressing, glossy leaves year-round beneath a tree. Happy in damp winter soils and drier conditions during summer, they require little care apart from the removal of old growth in spring.

*Bergenia cordifolia* **'Purpurea'** is a tall variety with cerise-pink flowers.

## FOXGLOVE *DIGITALIS PURPUREA*

**HEIGHT AND SPREAD** 5 ft × 18 in (1.5 m × 45 cm)
**SOIL** Any, except wet
**HARDINESS** Fully hardy
**SUN** ☼ ☀

This short-lived perennial lends a cottage-garden look to areas of dappled shade at the edge of a tree canopy. It produces a rosette of soft, oval leaves from which emerge tall spires of pink, purple, or white tubular flowers, loved by bees. Plants are easy to grow but may not bloom initially, producing leaves in the first year and flowers in the second summer. They die after flowering for a year or two but usually pop up again after self-seeding— if new plants do not appear, just buy more to fill the gaps.

**Foxgloves' tall spires** of tubular summer flowers thrive in dappled shade.

## MALE FERN *DRYOPTERIS FILIX-MAS*

**HEIGHT AND SPREAD** up to 4 × 3 ft (1.2 × 1 m)
**SOIL** Any, except wet
**HARDINESS** Fully hardy
**SUN** ☼ ☀

One of the easiest ferns to grow, *Dryopteris filix-mas* forms a clump of large leaves consisting of finely divided leaflets. Once established, it will grow happily beneath trees in the driest of soils and can be used to fill the gap in deep shade between the trunk and edge of the leaf canopy. The foliage often overwinters in sheltered spots, or may turn brown in cold areas; it is best removed in spring to make way for the new growth, which unfurls from arching stems, creating a feature at this time of year.

**The male fern** provides a sculptural feature in shady yards and requires little care.

# BARRENWORT *EPIMEDIUM*

**HEIGHT AND SPREAD** 12 × 20 in (30 × 50 cm)
**SOIL** Moist but well drained
**HARDINESS** Fully hardy
**SUN** ☼

This tough perennial tolerates many hours of shade each day, and its heart-shaped leaves will form a weed-suppressing carpet beneath a tree. The foliage of some species overwinters and the only job needed to keep this plant neat is to remove old leaves in early spring before the flowers appear. Good choices include *Epimedium × rubrum*, with its bronze-tinted young leaves and reddish-brown fall colors, and *E. × youngianum*, the foliage of which is bronze in spring and fall.

**Red barrenwort** (*Epimedium × rubrum*) has dainty blooms and is a useful ground cover plant.

# HELLEBORES *HELLEBORUS*

**HEIGHT AND SPREAD** up to 24 × 24 in (60 × 60 cm)
**SOIL** Any, apart from wet or acidic
**HARDINESS** Fully hardy
**SUN** ☼

Hellebores are versatile perennials that light up the winter and spring garden and require very little maintenance. Apart from Corsican hellebore (*Helleborus argutifolius*), they prefer light shade at the edge of a tree canopy and are happy in average soil, although they do not thrive in acid conditions (see p.12). For a display of blooms over many months, include the winter-flowering Christmas rose (*H. niger*) and some named hybrids in shades of pink, red, purple, yellow, or white. Remove any tattered old leaves in late winter.

*Helleborus × hybridus* **'Pluto'** has dark purple flowers from midwinter to mid-spring.

# WINTER ACONITE *ERANTHIS HYEMALIS*

**HEIGHT AND SPREAD** 4 × 6 in (10 × 15 cm)
**SOIL** Any, except wet
**HARDINESS** Fully hardy
**SUN** ☼ ☼

This diminutive plant produces sunny yellow flowers that are surrounded by a ruff of finely divided green foliage. It grows from a tuber, which you plant in the fall for flowers a few months later in mid to late winter, and thrives beneath the canopy of a deciduous tree, where sunlight can filter through the bare branches to the blooms below. Although it's not fussy, the best displays will be on soils that do not dry out completely in summer. If the conditions are right, this cold-season plant will flower annually with no maintenance.

**Sunny yellow** winter aconites brighten up the garden when few other plants are in bloom.

# DEADNETTLE *LAMIUM MACULATUM*

**HEIGHT AND SPREAD** 6 × 18 in (15 × 45 cm)
**SOIL** Any, except wet
**HARDINESS** Fully hardy
**SUN** ☼ ☼

Ideal for a woodland floor, this low-growing perennial will grow in the deep shade beneath a tree in full leaf. The two-toned green and silver foliage lightens up the gloom, and from late spring to early summer, small pink or white hooded flowers appear above it, adding an extra point of interest. Very easy to grow, deadnettle prefers moist soil but is also tolerant of dry conditions and rarely, if ever, needs watering once established. Trim back the stems in spring if they outgrow their allotted space.

**The flowers** of *Lamium maculatum* 'White Nancy' will glow in the shade beneath a tree.

# OREGON GRAPE *MAHONIA × MEDIA*

**HEIGHT AND SPREAD** 10 × 10 ft (3 × 3 m)
**SOIL** Any, except wet
**HARDINESS** Hardy to 5°C (−15°C)
**SUN** ☼ ☀

An evergreen shrub that offers year-round interest in a small woodland setting, the Oregon grape sports long, spiny leaves and, in late winter, sprays of small, highly scented, pollen-rich yellow flowers, followed by purple-blue berries. It grows slowly and may never reach its potential height if planted in full shade. While it tolerates most soils, it does best in a site sheltered from cold winds. Once established it needs no further care, apart from the occasional removal of dead stems after flowering.

**The evergreen** Oregon grape offers year-round color and interest beneath a tree canopy.

# SHIELD FERN *POLYSTICHUM*

**HEIGHT AND SPREAD** up to 4 × 4 ft (1.2 × 1.2 m)
**SOIL** Any, except wet
**HARDINESS** Fully hardy
**SUN** ☼ ☀

The shield fern is an excellent candidate for a small woodland, its evergreen (semi-evergreen in colder climes) arching fronds creating a beautiful textural effect in the shade beneath a tree. Soft shield fern (*Polystichum setiferum*) is slightly taller than hard shield fern (*P. aculeatum*), which grows to about 3 ft (90 cm). Both thrive in most soils; they dislike very wet conditions, but these rarely occur under a mature tree. Once established, the only care needed is the removal of old leaves in spring.

**The hard shield fern** (*Polystichum aculeatum*) thrives in the deep shade and dry soil beneath a tree.

# LUNGWORT *PULMONARIA*

**HEIGHT AND SPREAD** 12 × 8 in (30 × 20 cm)
**SOIL** Any, except wet
**HARDINESS** Fully hardy
**SUN** ☼ ☀

Grown for its large, spotted foliage that hugs the ground and suppresses weeds, this little perennial also bears leafy upright stems topped with funnel-shaped flowers, loved by bees. The spring blooms are pink when they open but soon change to blue, creating a two-tone effect. You can also buy white cultivars such as 'Sissinghurst White'. Happy in most soils and the deep shade under a tree, lungwort requires little care once established—just remove old or damaged foliage in spring and any unwanted seedlings.

**Easy-to-grow** *Pulmonaria* 'Lewis Palmer' bears bee-friendly pink and blue blooms.

# FRINGE CUPS *TELLIMA GRANDIFLORA*

**HEIGHT AND SPREAD** 30 × 12 in (75 × 30 cm)
**SOIL** Any, except wet
**HARDINESS** Fully hardy
**SUN** ☼ ☀

Fringe cups is a reliable perennial that will produce clumps of scalloped, rounded semi-evergreen leaves in the shade beneath a tree. The tall stems of small, greenish-yellow or cream flowers appear in late spring and early summer and often fade to red, producing a two-tone effect. Tolerant of both moist and dry soils, fringe cups only require you to cut back the old foliage in spring to keep it tidy. It will self-seed, but if you have enough plants you can prevent this by removing faded flower heads.

**The stems of fringe cups** are dotted with small flowers for many weeks from late spring.

# USING YOUR VERTICAL SPACE

**Walls and fences covered with foliage and flowers offer many benefits, particularly in small spaces where climbing plants take up little space on the ground. You can also introduce height using other structures, such as pergolas and arches, to create beautiful features that will be easy to care for if you choose well-behaved plants (see pp.52–55) and install appropriate supports to allow them to climb.**

*Clematis montana* is a large, easy-care climber that will cover a boundary wall or fence with flowers in late spring.

## CHOOSING CLIMBERS

Your plant choices are key to creating a beautiful low-maintenance vertical feature, for while some will cover their supports without any fuss, others may outgrow their allotted space in no time at all. For example, it may be tempting to select a fast-growing climber such as mile-a-minute (*Fallopia baldschuanica*) to cover a fence or old shed, but that plant will continue to grow quickly throughout its lifetime, so will need cutting back regularly to keep it in check. When selecting a climber for a boundary or freestanding feature, always check its final height and spread first to ensure your choice is suitable (*see pp.52–55 for examples*) and look for clues in a plant's profile, avoiding those described as "vigorous" or "fast-spreading" if you have only a small space to cover.

Also consider how the plant climbs and whether it needs wires, trellis, or other supports (*see opposite*). Providing a sturdy framework will pay dividends in the long run, allowing many climbers to grow away with little help from you.

**Compact honeysuckles**, such as 'Scentsation', create a screen of scented flowers on a wall in a small space.

## COOL STRUCTURES

Pergolas or arches that cover seating areas provide welcome shade in hot, sunny spaces, especially when enveloped with leafy plants that cool the air naturally and more effectively than artificial materials. You can also position these structures strategically to shade a flowerbed at the hottest times of the day, which will reduce evaporation rates and therefore watering requirements—just check that the plants in the bed can cope with lower light levels.

Consider the materials your pergolas and arches are made from, too. Arches constructed from stainless steel will be durable, but climbers such as clematis will find them difficult to scale if the posts are smooth with a wide circumference. Wrapping chicken wire around them would help solve the problem, but wood is perhaps a better material choice if you affix wires or trellis to it, as most climbers will scramble up these. Products made from FSC-certified hardwood, which is sourced from sustainably managed forests, will not require painting or preservatives.

**For a display** of summer flowers, train a climbing rose on the wired posts and overhead beams of a wooden pergola.

## CLIMBING METHODS

Climbers use a range of methods to haul themselves up. The easiest climbers for the low-maintenance gardener are the self-clinging types, such as ivy, Boston ivy, Virginia creeper (*Parthenocissus* species), and climbing hydrangea. These employ either stem roots or adhesive pads to cling to their supports and require no wires or trellis.

Twiners such as clematis and passion flower (*Passiflora*) use leaf stalks and tendrils to cling to their supports, while honeysuckle (*Lonicera*) and star jasmine (*Trachelospermum*) have twining stems. Climbing roses make their ascent by hooking their thorny stems onto their host. Ideal supports for twiners and roses include bamboo canes, trellis, wires, and shrub or tree stems. Twiners will grow unaided once attached to their

**Thin mesh** affixed securely to a fence will be strong enough to support the twining leaf stalks of a small clematis.

supports, as will roses grown through shrubs and trees, but rose stems trained onto wires or trellis will need to be tied to these supports once or twice a year.

## WIRING UP

Use the same method to affix wires horizontally to a fence or wall or vertically to the posts of a pergola or arch. For a fence, install eye screws at 18 in (45 cm) intervals vertically up one fence post and then repeat up an adjacent post; for a wall, install eye screws vertically at the same intervals and repeat about 6 ft (1.8 m) apart. Thread thick-gauge wire through the first eye and twist the ends to secure it, and then attach it to its horizontally

corresponding eye. Pull the wire taut, twist around the second eye, and secure. For a pergola or arch, add four eyes to the top of each side of a vertical post and four corresponding eyes at the bottom, and attach the wire between them as described above.

Attach twiners to the wires initially using soft string—they will then climb of their own accord. Bend flexible rose stems along the horizontal wires on a fence or wall and tie them in place with string or plant ties. Training them in this way produces more flowers.

**Pull wire taut** between upper and lower eye screws on a pergola or rose arch and secure by twisting the ends as shown.

**Clematis and other twiners' stems** will need to be tied on to the wires initially but will then climb up of their own accord.

# EASY CLIMBING PLANTS

Climbing plants help to soften the hard edges of walls, fences, and structures such as pergolas and arches with veils of foliage and flowers. Choose evergreens for year-round color and deciduous types that bloom in different seasons for a long-lasting show. The plants on these pages are easy to care for, requiring just a little attention once or twice a year in exchange for a profusion of colors and textures. Check that those you select will fit your space or structure, and remember to install the supports they require before planting them.

## CHOCOLATE VINE *AKEBIA QUINATA*

**HEIGHT AND SPREAD** up to 25 × 6 ft (8 × 2 m)
**SOIL** Moist but well drained
**HARDINESS** Fully hardy
**SUN** ☼ ☀

The chocolate vine is a vigorous, twining, semi-evergreen climber, ideal for growing through a tree, along a fence or wall, or over a large pergola. It produces bright green divided leaves, which often persist through winter in mild areas, and dark red spring flowers with a spicy scent. The blooms may be followed by long purple fruits if you have two plants that can cross-pollinate. Easy to grow, it just needs a small-gauge trellis, wires, or a tree to twine around. Trim it after flowering as required.

**The chocolate vine's** lightly scented, dark red flowers open amid bright green foliage.

## CLEMATIS 'JACKMANII'

**HEIGHT AND SPREAD** up to 10 × 3 ft (3 × 1 m)
**SOIL** Moist but well drained, alkaline or neutral
**HARDINESS** Fully hardy
**SUN** ☼ ☀

This large-flowered plant and other cultivars in the same group, such as JACKMANII PURPUREA, are among the most reliable clematis and flower from midsummer to early fall. 'Jackmanii' produces deep purple, velvety blooms and is a good choice for growing over a rose arch or up a trellis panel. Plant the crown (where the roots meet the stems) 2 in (5 cm) below the surface in some shade. In early spring, trim back all the stems to strong buds 6–8 in (15–20 cm) above the ground and apply a mulch.

**JACKMANII PURPUREA** is a reddish-purple cultivar of the original purple form.

## MOUNTAIN CLEMATIS *CLEMATIS MONTANA*

**HEIGHT AND SPREAD** 20 × 15 ft (6 × 5 m)
**SOIL** Moist but well drained, alkaline or neutral
**HARDINESS** Fully hardy
**SUN** ☼ ☀

The mountain clematis is a reliable early-flowering species, with white, lightly scented flowers, pink in some cultivars, that last from late spring to early summer. It is a large plant and makes a beautiful feature when woven through a tree or trained on horizontal wires affixed to a wall or fence. Easy to grow, it requires no pruning, apart from trimming stems that have outgrown their allotted space after flowering. The sturdy stems are often bare at the base but can be disguised with other planting.

*Clematis montana* var. *grandiflora* has slightly larger flowers than the species.

## CLEMATIS 'NELLY MOSER'

**HEIGHT AND SPREAD** 10 × 3 ft (3 × 1 m)
**SOIL** Moist but well drained, alkaline or neutral
**HARDINESS** Fully hardy
**SUN** ☀

One of the most reliable of the large-flowered clematis, in early summer 'Nelly Moser' produces an abundance of pink-striped flowers, loved by bees and butterflies. It is perfect for a shady wall or trained over a pergola or arch where its flowers won't fade in strong sun. Annual care is minimal: simply cut back dead and damaged growth in early spring, and trim the remaining stems back to the first or second strong bud from the top. Apply a mulch of garden compost around the base at the same time.

**'Nelly Moser'** is a reliable cultivar, producing pink-striped blooms in early summer.

## CLEMATIS 'NIOBE'

**HEIGHT AND SPREAD** 8 × 3 ft (2.5 × 1 m)
**SOIL** Moist but well drained, alkaline or neutral
**HARDINESS** Fully hardy
**SUN** ☀ ☀

This relatively compact, large-flowered clematis is loved for its velvety, ruby-red flowers, which appear in early summer, often with a second flush later in the season. A reliable cultivar, happy in sun or part shade, it is perfect for a pillar, a trellis panel on a wall, or an arch. Like all clematis that flower at this time, it needs just a light prune in early spring, when the stems should be cut down to the first or second healthy bud from the top. Apply a mulch of well-rotted garden compost each spring.

**Red, velvety flowers** adorn 'Niobe' in early summer, with a second flush in late summer.

## GOLDEN CLEMATIS *CLEMATIS TANGUTICA*

**HEIGHT AND SPREAD** up to 20 × 10 ft (6 × 3 m)
**SOIL** Moist but well drained, alkaline or neutral
**HARDINESS** Fully hardy
**SUN** ☀ ☀

The golden clematis produces scrambling stems that quickly climb through a large shrub or tree, or cover a wired fence or wall, decorating their supports with divided leaves and yellow, lantern-shaped flowers from summer to fall. Decorative seed heads follow the blooms and last all winter. 'Bill MacKenzie' is one of the most popular cultivars, with slightly larger flowers. Simply cut all the stems down to about 8 in (20 cm) from the ground in early spring, and add a mulch of well-rotted compost.

**Perfect for beginners,** the golden clematis needs just a quick prune once a year.

## PURPLE CLEMATIS *CLEMATIS VITICELLA*

**HEIGHT AND SPREAD** up to 10 × 5 ft (3 × 1.5 m)
**SOIL** Moist but well drained, alkaline or neutral
**HARDINESS** Fully hardy
**SUN** ☀ ☀

Despite their common name, not all of these late-flowering clematis are purple—cultivars also come in pink and white. Popular varieties include the dark purple 'Etoile Violette', pink 'Purpurea Plena Elegans', and white 'Alba Luxurians'. Disease-resistant and reliable, these plants produce dainty, bell-shaped or round blooms from midsummer. Grow them through shrubs, on trellis, a wired wall or fence, or over an arch. Cut the stems down to 8 in (20 cm) from the ground in early spring, and add a mulch.

**'Purpurea Plena Elegans'** is a pink double-flowered form that blooms for many weeks.

## CLIMBING HYDRANGEA

**HYDRANGEA ANOMALA SUBSP. PETIOLARIS**

**HEIGHT AND SPREAD** up to 40 × 10 ft (12 × 3 m)
**SOIL** Any, except wet
**HARDINESS** Hardy to 5°F (−15°C)
**SUN** ☼ ☼ ☀

This versatile deciduous climber has sturdy stems that cling via aerial roots and require no assistance to adhere to a support. Once it is established, leave it to its own devices, or encourage the stems to travel horizontally to cover a fence or wall with its oval green leaves and showy white summer flower heads. Snip off the old flowers, remove unwanted stems, and apply a mulch of well-rotted organic matter in spring.

**The white,** flat-topped flower heads of the climbing hydrangea stand out against the dark green leaves.

## CHINESE VIRGINIA CREEPER

**PARTHENOCISSUS HENRYANA**

**HEIGHT AND SPREAD** up to 40 × 12 ft (12 × 4 m)
**SOIL** Any, except wet
**HARDINESS** Hardy to 5°F (−15°C)
**SUN** ☼ ☼ ☀

One of the least vigorous of the *Parthenocissus* species, Chinese Virginia creeper is ideal for covering a shady fence or wall, clinging of its own accord with small disklike suckers. Its handsome, divided leaves are decorated with silvery veins and fire up in the fall, producing a scarlet screen punctuated with dark blue berries. Trim back unwanted growth in early spring and add a mulch of well-rotted compost on very dry soils.

**The handsome leaves** of this Virginia creeper turn red before dropping in fall.

## COMMON HONEYSUCKLE *LONICERA PERICLYMENUM*

**HEIGHT AND SPREAD** 22 × 3 ft (7 × 1 m)
**SOIL** Moist but free-draining
**HARDINESS** Fully hardy
**SUN** ☼ ☼

A deciduous twining climber grown for its sweetly fragrant tubular flowers, which appear from summer to early fall, this cottage-garden favorite is easy to train along a wall or fence, over a pergola, or through a large shrub or tree. Pollinating moths are drawn to the evening-scented blooms, which come in shades of pink or yellow and white. Red berries follow the flowers. Provide wires or trellis for the stems to cling to and cut back the flowering stems by a third in late summer. Apply a mulch of rotted compost in spring.

**The cultivar 'Serotina'** has highly fragrant reddish-purple and white blooms.

## *ROSA* 'BOBBY JAMES'

**HEIGHT AND SPREAD** 20 × 12 ft (6 × 4 m)
**SOIL** Any, except wet
**HARDINESS** Fully hardy
**SUN** ☼ ☼

The rambling rose 'Bobby James' produces large clusters of small, white, highly fragrant flowers in summer among disease-resistant green leaves. The easiest way to grow it is through a mature tree, where, after the stems are tied to a trellis or canes angled toward the trunk, they will reach up into the canopy unaided. Cut out dead or diseased growth after flowering, and renovate old plants in winter by cutting all the stems down to the base, bar 4–6 young healthy ones. In spring, apply a mulch of well-rotted compost.

**'Bobby James'** will decorate a mature tree with its climbing stems of scented white flowers.

## ROSA 'COMPASSION'

**HEIGHT AND SPREAD** 10 x 10ft (3 x 3m)
**SOIL** Any, except wet
**HARDINESS** Fully hardy
**SUN** ☀

Perfect for a pergola or arch, or a wired fence or wall, this disease-resistant rose produces glossy, dark green foliage and scented, apricot-pink flowers in summer and early fall. Red hips follow the blooms. Like all climbing roses, the stems must be tied to a sturdy support; training them horizontally will produce more blooms. In winter, remove dead, diseased, and weak stems, tie in new stems, and shorten side shoots by two-thirds. Apply a rose fertilizer and mulch in early spring.

**'Compassion'** is an award-winning climber with scented, apricot-pink summer flowers.

## ROSA 'CONSTANCE SPRY'

**HEIGHT AND SPREAD** up to 8 x 8ft (2.5 x 2.5m)
**SOIL** Any, except wet
**HARDINESS** Fully hardy
**SUN** ☀ ☀

This beautiful climber flowers just once in early summer but puts on a magnificent show, its scented pink blooms making an invaluable contribution to a pergola or wired wall or fence. Renowned for its healthy foliage and disease resistance, it will also grow in a little shade. Water well as it establishes, and in winter remove any dead, damaged, or weak stems. Tie in the new stems to their support and prune back the side-stems by two-thirds to a healthy bud. Add a rose fertilizer and mulch in early spring.

**Scented pink roses** adorn the stems of 'Constance Spry' in early summer.

## ROSA 'NEW DAWN'

**HEIGHT AND SPREAD** up to 8 x 8ft (2.5 x 2.5m)
**SOIL** Any, except wet
**HARDINESS** Fully hardy
**SUN** ☀ ☀

When grown over a pergola or arch or on a wall or fence, this repeat-flowering climber will reward you with dark green, glossy foliage and a profusion of lightly scented, pearly pink flowers from summer to early fall. It is relatively compact and can also be grown up a pillar. Water well until established, and apply a rose fertilizer and mulch annually in early spring. To prune it, simply remove any dead, diseased, and weak stems in winter, and cut the side stems back by two-thirds.

**The pearly pink,** lightly scented flowers of 'New Dawn' bloom through the summer and early fall.

## STAR JASMINE *TRACHELOSPERMUM JASMINOIDES*

**HEIGHT AND SPREAD** 12 x12ft (4 x 4m)
**SOIL** Well drained
**HARDINESS** Hardy to 14°F (−10°C)
**SUN** ☀ ☀

A good choice for a warm, sheltered space, star jasmine is an evergreen twining climber that will scramble along wires on a wall, fence, or pergola, or up a trellis. Its small, dark green foliage turns deep red in winter, and highly scented, white, starry flowers appear in summer. Grow it close to a seating area or the entrance to your space to welcome guests with its perfume. Easy to grow, it's very drought-tolerant and will only need pruning in late summer, after it has flowered, to keep the stems in check.

**Star jasmine's flowers** may be small, but they emit a strong and beautiful perfume.

**Cultivated blackberries** are among the easiest fruit crops to grow and will only need your care once a year to deliver their bounty.

# EASY EDIBLES

**Fruit and vegetable plots can be very time-consuming if you plant crops that require protection from pests or succumb easily to diseases. However, there are some edible plants that will produce a plateful of delicious food with the minimum of fuss. Planting them in the right place and at the right time will help deliver a good harvest, while ensuring that your site and soil conditions suit your crops will also guarantee high yields with little effort from you.**

# MAKING A SIMPLE PRODUCTIVE BED

Growing your own fruit and vegetables can be easy if you choose your crops carefully and enrich the soil so that it provides your edibles with the moisture and nutrients they need. Young vegetable plants need frequent watering, so make time for this task or install an automatic watering system. Avoid siting your bed in a windy spot or where it will receive more than six or seven hours of sun each day.

**If you have poor, dusty, or wet soil,** grow your vegetables in a raised bed filled with topsoil mixed with some compost.

**Swiss chard and other leafy crops** grow well in part shade, where the soil will remain moist for longer than in sunny beds.

## LOCATING A BED

Creating a productive bed to grow a few fruit and vegetable crops couldn't be easier. Simply follow the advice for creating an ornamental bed (see pp.22–23) or make one in a raised bed (see pp.34–35). When choosing a location for your productive space, bear in mind that many crops require a sunny site, and you will need to water vegetable plants regularly unless rainfall suffices, so choose an area close to an outside tap or rain barrel to make this task easier. Creating a bed next to a path will allow you to transport compost, plants, and your harvests more easily in a wheelbarrow so that you won't have to carry them far. Avoid areas in a rain shadow next to a wall or fence, where the soil will be very dry and crops will struggle.

The size of your productive bed will be determined by what you plan to plant. A few lettuces, radishes, and beets can be squeezed into a small bed of about 2 ft (60 cm) square or less, but larger plants, such as tomatoes and peppers, will need at least a square yard (meter). Check the vegetables on pp.62–65 and fruits on pp.72–73 for a selection of easy crops.

## IMPROVING THE SOIL

Most crops are hungry feeders and need a soil rich in nutrients that holds sufficient water for rapid growth but also drains well so that their roots do not rot. The best way to achieve this perfect balance is to add a 2 in (5 cm) layer of organic matter (mulch) such as well-rotted manure from a reliable, organic source or garden compost over your bed. Apply the mulch in the fall if you have heavy clay soil or in early spring if you have light sandy soil (see pp.12–13). Even a loam soil will benefit from a mulch to maintain its productivity and help reduce weed growth.

While mulches are not packed with as many nutrients as fertilizers, they attract worms and other soil-borne creatures to your plot to feed on the organic matter, and their casts (droppings) then enrich the soil (see also pp.132–133). Some plants, especially fruiting crops, may need a nutrient boost as they come into flower, but if your crops bloom well and you keep the soil moist, they should not need much feeding apart from the occasional dose of balanced organic fertilizer. You may also need to apply a nitrogen-rich fertilizer in summer if you are growing crops close together.

**Apply a thick layer** of organic matter over the soil to help increase its nutrient content and lock in moisture.

## WHEN TO PLANT

Some crops that mature quickly can be planted in succession every few weeks from spring through to summer to produce a long harvest. Hardy vegetable crops and fruit bushes, such as currants, blackberries, and raspberries, are best planted in the fall or spring, when rain will water them as they establish, saving you the job. However, climate change has brought with it unreliable weather patterns, so water all new plants during prolonged periods of drought, except in the depths of winter when their growth will be very slow. Beans, squashes, peppers, and tomatoes are not hardy and must only be planted outside after all risk of frost has passed in late spring or early summer (see also pp.60–61).

**Planting currant and berry bushes** in the fall will allow the winter rains to water them in, rather than you doing the job.

## SOWING SEED VS BUYING YOUNG PLANTS

The easiest and most reliable way of ensuring your vegetable crops deliver on their promise is to buy young plants, known as plugs, from a garden center or online nursery. However, your choice of varieties will be limited and the cost will be much higher than that for seeds. Sowing seeds is more time-consuming, but many easy crops will germinate quickly in pots of seed starting mix. Sown indoors on a windowsill or in a greenhouse, they will be protected from pests and some diseases, too. Small plug plants may also need to be potted on into larger containers before you plant them outside (see pp.60–61 for more growing advice).

**Sowing seed** is more time-consuming than buying young plants, but it offers you a greater choice of varieties.

**TOP TIP** WHEN SOWING SEEDS ON A WINDOWSILL INDOORS, TURN THE POTS OR TRAYS EVERY DAY OR TWO TO PREVENT THE SEEDLINGS BECOMING TALL, SPINDLY, AND WEAK AS THEY STRETCH TOWARD THE LIGHT.

# PLANTING AN EASY-CARE VEGETABLE BED

Before planting up your vegetable plot, take time to prepare the soil (*see p.59*) and remove the weeds, which will compete with your crops for water, nutrients, and light. To keep maintenance to a minimum, choose crops that are resistant to pest damage and diseases and can survive a little drought—or install an automatic watering system if you plan to grow thirsty crops such as beans.

**Harvests will be larger and easier** to achieve if you prepare your soil and remove weeds before you start.

## CHOOSING CROPS

When choosing what to plant in your productive bed, the best advice is to grow what you like to eat. You could also be adventurous and try crops that are not easy to buy in stores, such as mizuna (*see p.63*). When buying plug plants or seeds, look for varieties that are disease-resistant and check whether they are tender or hardy—tender crops will need to be cared for indoors before being planted outside after the frosts (*see right*).

**Tender plants** such as squashes must only be planted outside after the frosts.

### NEED TO KNOW

- Plants raised indoors need time to transition from the warmth of your home or greenhouse to the cooler temperatures outside. This process is known as "hardening off."
- To harden off seedlings and tender plants, place them outside in trays during the day for the last two weeks of spring but bring them inside at night to avoid any damage caused by late frosts.
- In early summer, once all risk of frost has passed, your seedlings can then be planted outside.

**The tubes of toilet paper rolls** make excellent biodegradable pots for crops with long roots such as beans.

## EASY POTS

Growing young plants or raising your seeds in biodegradable pots can make life easier when planting out, since you simply plant the pot with the crop. The pot will then rot down, allowing the plant's roots to reach out into the soil. These pots are available to buy, or you can make your own using the tubes of toilet paper rolls to house your seedlings. Pack the tubes into a rigid container such as a plastic fruit basket from the supermarket, so they keep their shape and potting mix does not escape from the bottom.

# HOW TO PLANT VEGETABLES

This small bed is just 5 x 5 ft (1.5 x 1.5 m), but you could make yours smaller or larger, depending on the available space.

**YOU WILL NEED** Spade and/or Dutch hoe • Mulch (see p.59) • String • Poles for beans • Sheet of black plastic or landscape fabric • Stones or bricks • Chosen seeds and/or seedlings

1 Remove all the weeds from your bed, digging out the roots from perennials such as dandelions and docks. Use a Dutch hoe to remove small weed seedlings: on a dry day, push the blade just below the soil surface to sever the leafy tops from the roots, leaving the weeds to wither on the surface. Then apply a mulch if you did not already do so in the fall.

2 Using string, divide the growing space into nine equal areas for each of your crops. If growing pole beans, create tripods or A-frames using 6 ft (1.8 m) canes as shown.

3 In early spring, warm up the soil by laying a sheet of black plastic or landscape fabric over the surface; use large stones to secure it. Then remove the covering to sow hardy seeds directly into the bed, or make holes in it and plant your seedlings through it to keep weeds at bay.

4 Before the frosts are over, plant up seedlings of hardy crops such as onions, radishes, beets, and lettuces. After the frosts, add tender types, including beans, sweet corn, squashes, and peppers.

5 Keep the crops well-watered as they establish—installing an automatic irrigation system (see p.79) may be the best option if you are growing thirsty crops such as squashes.

6 Pull out or hoe off any weeds that germinate around your crops—they should be easy to remove from the mulch—and protect vulnerable crops from slug and snail damage (see *also pp.136–137 for tips on pest control*).

# EASY CROPS FOR SMALL SPACES

The edibles on these pages are among the easiest crops to grow and should provide a harvest without too much effort. Many vegetables can be raised from seed each year, although buying small seedling plants at a garden center saves time. This selection is also perfect for growing in a raised bed (*see pp.34–35*) and some are suitable for containers—just be prepared to water crops in pots more than those in the ground.

## SALAD ONIONS *ALLIUM FISTULOSUM*

**HEIGHT AND SPREAD** up to 12 × 2 in (30 × 5 cm)
**SOIL** Free-draining
**HARDINESS** Fully hardy
**SUN** ☼ ☼

Even easier to grow than regular onions, these crops can be raised in the ground or in a container filled with peat-free potting mix. Sow seed thinly in rows 4 in (10 cm) apart every two weeks from spring to fall for a continuous harvest. There is no need to thin the seedlings as you will be harvesting the onions before they get too big. Water during dry spells and the crops should be ready to eat about eight weeks after sowing, when they are about 6 in (15 cm) tall.

**Salad or spring onions** are ready to harvest just eight weeks after sowing the seeds.

## ONIONS *ALLIUM CEPA*

**HEIGHT AND SPREAD** up to 30 × 24 in (75 × 60 cm)
**SOIL** Free-draining
**HARDINESS** Hardy
**SUN** ☼

Onions are easy to grow from sets (small bulbs). In spring, plant them 2–4 in (5–10 cm) apart, with 10 in (25 cm) between rows, ensuring the pointed tips are just above the surface. Cover with fleece to prevent bird damage until the plants are established. During dry weather, water the soil around the sets every 14 days until midsummer, avoiding wetting the plants. Lift the bulbs from late summer to early fall when the foliage turns yellow but before it dies down completely.

**'Red Baron'** is a red-skinned onion with disease- and bolt-resistance and a great flavor.

## WILD GARLIC *ALLIUM URSINUM*

**HEIGHT AND SPREAD** 12 × 12 in (30 × 30 cm)
**SOIL** Moist but free-draining
**HARDINESS** Fully hardy
**SUN** ☼ ☼

Wild garlic, or ramson, is an easy-care woodland perennial that belongs to the same family as garlic bulbs. The tasty young leaves are delicious in salads and pesto sauces, while mature foliage can be steamed. In the fall, sow seeds at the edge of a tree canopy, where they would grow in the wild, and wait for them to germinate in spring. Plants reappear annually, but die down in summer. Wild garlic can self-seed prolifically, so keep it in check by harvesting the edible flowers for use in salads.

**Ideal for shady areas** unsuitable for most crops, wild garlic will thrive beneath a deciduous tree.

## SWISS CHARD

*BETA VULGARIS* SUBSP. *CICLA* VAR. *FLAVESCENS*

**HEIGHT AND SPREAD** 18 × 18 in (45 × 45 cm)
**SOIL** Well drained
**HARDINESS** Fully hardy
**SUN** ☼ ☼

Also known as leaf beet, Swiss chard produces colorful stems of green leaves in summer. These can be eaten raw in salads, steamed, or boiled. In spring, sow seeds thinly into drills ¾ in (2 cm) deep, cover with soil, and water in. Alternatively, sow into containers of peat-free potting mix. When seedlings have a few leaves, thin to 12 in (30 cm) apart. Keep plants watered and harvest the leaves from midsummer.

**The colorful stems** of Swiss chard add a decorative touch to a productive garden bed.

## MIZUNA *BRASSICA RAPA* SUBSP. *NIPPOSINICA*

**HEIGHT AND SPREAD** up to 10 × 10 in (25 × 25 cm)
**SOIL** Moist but free-draining
**HARDINESS** Fully hardy
**SUN** ☼ ☼

Often grown alongside mibuna, this similar Japanese leafy crop can be used in salads and stir-fries. Sowing small batches of seed every few weeks from early spring to midsummer will generate a long harvest. Sow seed thinly in rows, then thin the seedlings so they are 6–8 in (15–20 cm) apart. Keep plants well watered to prevent them from "bolting" (flowering). If slugs eat the seedlings, try sowing in containers of peat-free potting mix that you can protect more easily.

**Mizuna** has a peppery taste, and the individual leaves can be harvested over a long period.

## BEETS *BETA VULGARIS* SUBSP. *VULGARIS*

**HEIGHT AND SPREAD** 12 × 8 in (30 × 20 cm)
**SOIL** Well drained
**HARDINESS** Fully hardy
**SUN** ☼ ☼

These delicious roots are easy to grow in a bed or in containers. Add a mulch of well-rotted garden compost to beds in early spring. In mid-spring, sow 2–3 seeds in one spot in holes 1 in (2.5 cm) deep and 4 in (10 cm) apart. After germination, remove the weakest seedlings and use in salads. Sow small batches every couple of weeks for a succession of crops. Water your plants regularly and harvest when the roots are about the size of a golf ball—larger roots may be woody.

**Beets** are sweet and tender when they are the approximate size of a golf ball.

## CHILE PEPPER *CAPSICUM FRUTESCENS*

**HEIGHT AND SPREAD** 24 × 20 in (60 × 50 cm)
**GROWING MEDIUM** Peat-free potting mix
**HARDINESS** Hardy to 46°F (8°C)
**SUN** ☼

Chile plants produce hot-flavored fruits that are both delicious and ornamental. While it is possible to raise chile peppers from seed, the easiest option is to buy young plants in spring and plant them in containers of potting mix. Chiles are tender and should not be set outside until daytime temperatures are consistently above 61°F (16°C). Alternatively, grow indoors on a windowsill. Pinch out the shoot tips to encourage more fruiting stems and keep plants well watered. Use canes to support fruit-laden stems.

**'NuMex Twilight'** produces medium-hot, slender fruits that change color as they mature.

## KOHLRABI *BRASSICA OLERACEA* (GONGYLODES GROUP)

**HEIGHT AND SPREAD** 18 × 18 in (45 × 45 cm)
**SOIL** Moist but well drained
**HARDINESS** Fully hardy
**SUN** ☼ ☼

These sweet mini cabbage–like green or purple crops are easy to grow and ideal for small plots. Sow the seed in batches from spring to summer for a long harvest. Sow directly into a prepared bed, and when the seedlings are about 1 in (2.5 cm) tall, thin to a final spacing of 6–8 in (15–20 cm). Water during dry spells and cover plants with fleece to prevent bird and cabbage root fly attacks. Harvest kohlrabi when they are the size of a golf or tennis ball and steam them or grate them in salads.

**Sow seeds** every few weeks for a long harvest of kohlrabi roots from summer to fall.

## SUMMER SPINACH *CHENOPODIUM GIGANTEUM*

**HEIGHT AND SPREAD** up to 6 × 3 ft (2 × 1 m)
**SOIL** Well drained
**HARDINESS** Hardy to 5°F (−15°C)
**SUN** ☼ ☼

A trouble-free and easy-to-grow alternative to ordinary spinach, this majestic plant produces a colorful crop which also makes a decorative feature in a border if you have no space for a vegetable bed. Cook it like spinach or add raw young leaves to salads. Sow the seeds indoors in pots in early spring and plant outside at the back of a bed after the frosts. Water plants well until established, after which they will be quite drought-tolerant. Summer spinach needs no feeding, but will self-seed if allowed to flower.

**The young pink shoots** of summer spinach are loaded with nutrients and flavor.

## ZUCCHINI *CUCURBITA PEPO*

**HEIGHT AND SPREAD** 32 × 32 in (80 × 80 cm)
**SOIL** Moist but well drained
**HARDINESS** Hardy to 46°F (8°C)
**SUN** ☼

Zucchini are very easy to grow, and just two plants will produce fruits for a family. In early spring, sow two seeds in each pot of seed-starting mix and place on a sunny windowsill until they germinate. Remove the weakest seedlings when they have a few leaves. Grow on indoors until all risk of frost has passed. Plant out 3 ft (90 cm) apart in a bed enriched with garden compost or large containers of peat-free potting mix. To prevent disease, avoid wetting the leaves.

**A layer of straw** will help prevent zucchini fruits rotting on wet soil in a bed.

## LETTUCE *LACTUCA SATIVA*

**HEIGHT AND SPREAD** up to 10 × 10 in (25 × 25 cm)
**SOIL** Peat-free multipurpose
**HARDINESS** Hardy to 23°F (−5°C)
**SUN** ☼ ☼

Sowing lettuce seeds in pots raised off the ground is a great way to grow salad leaves while protecting the young plants from slugs and snails, which often munch their way through crops in the ground. From mid-spring, sow seed in shallow drills and cover with compost. Leave the seedlings to grow on if you plan to use them as cut-and-come-again leaves (see p.97), or thin the plants to 6–8 in (15–20 cm) apart if you want mature heads. Keep plants well-watered.

**'Lollo Rossa'** is a loose-leaf lettuce that can be used as a cut-and-come-again crop or left to mature into a full head.

## SNOW PEAS *PISUM SATIVUM* VAR. *SACCHARATUM*

**HEIGHT AND SPREAD** up to 36 × 12 in (90 × 30 cm)
**SOIL** Moist but free-draining
**HARDINESS** Hardy to 28°F (–2°C)
**SUN** ☼

Also known as sugar snap peas, these edible pods of immature peas are eaten steamed, boiled, or raw in salads. In late spring, make a flat-bottomed trench 2 in (5 cm) deep and 6 in (15 cm) wide and sow the seeds into it, 3 in (7.5 cm) apart. Cover with soil and add fleece to deter pigeons, which are among the few pests that attack this crop. Push in tall, twiggy shrub prunings or erect netting attached to bamboo canes for the stems to climb up. Pick the pods regularly when mature.

**Snow peas** are easier to grow than regular peas, but their scrambling stems will need some support.

## EARLY POTATOES *SOLANUM TUBEROSUM*

**HEIGHT AND SPREAD** up to 30 × 24 in (75 × 60 cm)
**SOIL** Moist but free-draining
**HARDINESS** Hardy to 34°F (1°C)
**SUN** ☼

Early potatoes are the best choice where blight disease is a problem (see p.139). In early spring, stand seed potatoes in an egg crate with the dents facing up. Set on a windowsill to "chit" (sprout shoots). Once the shoots are 1¼ in (3 cm) tall, rub off all except four per tuber. Plant out in trenches 6 in (15 cm) deep and 18 in (45 cm) apart. When the shoots are 4 in (10 cm) tall, cover them with soil to protect them from frost and to encourage heavier crops. Repeat twice more, then leave the plants to grow on.

**Mounding soil** around potato stems, known as "hilling up," encourages a heavy crop.

## RADISH *RAPHANUS SATIVUS*

**HEIGHT AND SPREAD** 6 × 4 in (15 × 10 cm)
**SOIL** Moist but well drained
**HARDINESS** Fully hardy
**SUN** ☼ ☼

Delicious in salads, radishes can be sown in batches every couple of weeks from spring to late summer for a long harvest. A few weeks before sowing in spring, add a mulch of well-rotted garden compost over your bed. Sow seed 1 in (2.5 cm) apart in shallow drills and cover with soil. Keep plants moist to prevent them "bolting" (flowering) and apply a seaweed feed when they are growing well. The roots will grow just above the soil and should be ready for pulling and eating 4–6 weeks after sowing.

**'French Breakfast'** radishes are cylindrical in shape and add a hot, spicy flavor to salads.

## CORN *ZEA MAYS*

**HEIGHT AND SPREAD** up to 5 × 1¾ ft (1.5 × 0.5 m)
**SOIL** Moist but well drained
**HARDINESS** Hardy to 41°F (5°C)
**SUN** ☼

Easy to grow, tender corn cobs are delicious when picked straight from the garden. Start off the seeds indoors in spring, or buy seedlings from a garden center, and grow them on in pots on a windowsill until all risk of frost has passed. Then plant the seedlings outside in a sunny, sheltered spot about 18 in (45 cm) apart in a grid formation to aid wind pollination. Mulch the soil and water plants during dry spells. Harvest when the tassels turn brown and the kernels release a milky liquid when pressed.

**Planting corn** in a grid formation allows the wind to pollinate the flowers more easily.

# GROWING HERBS FOR THE KITCHEN

Herbs comprise a wide range of plants, including species such as lavender and marigolds that were traditionally used to treat mild ailments, but are now grown more for their flowers. However, the plants most people regard as herbs today are those used as flavorings, such as sage and thyme, which are easy to grow in pots or in the ground and provide a range of leaves and flowers for your kitchen.

**Elegant bay trees** are easy to grow in a sunny or partly shaded yard, and produce reliable crops of leaves each year.

## WHERE TO GROW HERBS

The first step into gardening for many people is growing a few herbs in a pot by the kitchen door or on a windowsill, and because most of these plants are happy in dry soil, they thrive in their containers. However, as is the case with nearly all plants, an even easier way to grow herbs is in the ground, where they will rarely, if ever, need watering or feeding once established, although some may benefit from an annual trim to keep them bushy and compact. The exception to this rule is if you have heavy clay soil that is prone to waterlogging in winter. Cold, wet soil will rot the stems of drought-lovers such as thyme, sage, and rosemary, but growing them in raised beds will cure the problem. Most herbs also need a bright position with at least six hours of direct sun each day in summer. In shadier spots, grow mint, chives, and oregano, which tolerate lower light conditions. Planting herbs in beds next to a patio or path will make them easy to harvest.

**Culinary herbs** such as thyme and sage create an aromatic edging for a sunny border next to a path or patio.

**Thyme grows well in a pot** and needs less watering if you cover the potting mix with gravel to conserve moisture.

## PLANTING IN POTS

While it is more time-consuming to cultivate herbs in pots, you may find this is the most convenient way to grow them close to the house, so it is easy to pop out for some leaves. You can grow a selection in an herb pot, which is a large terra-cotta container with holes around the sides. These pots are best suited to compact, drought-tolerant herbs such as thyme and chives that are happy with low levels of moisture, as water often spills out of the top holes before percolating down to the plants below.

Most shrubby or perennial herbs will live longer in a simple large container at least 8 in (20 cm) deep with drainage holes at the bottom. Fill it with an enriched potting mix with added perlite mixed in for extra drainage. Leave a gap of about 2 in (5 cm) between the pot rim and the top of the potting mix, once the herbs have been planted, to allow space for water to collect. Water once a week, or twice during a hot summer. In spring, remove some of the potting mix and replace it with fresh mix with some added granular fertilizer.

## CHOOSING HERBS

Select some easy-care herbs from the directory on pp.68–69, opting for compact types such as thyme, sage, and chives for a large pot of mixed flavors (*see also advice on mint below*). Larger herbs, including rosemary and bay, are best grown in the ground if you don't want to repot them every few years. Some sages may also outgrow their containers after a few years, when you could transfer them to the front of a sunny flowerbed to form an aromatic, evergreen edible edging.

Herbs such as the annuals basil and cilantro, and biennial parsley, can be grown from seed each spring, but this is time-consuming and some, most notably basil, can be very fussy and difficult to grow if the temperature and soil are not to their liking. If you love these herbs, consider buying young plants from the garden center each year to avoid disappointment.

**Thyme is very easy** to grow in a bed of free-draining soil, and there are many different varieties and flavors available.

## PLANTING AND HARVESTING

Always plant herbs at the same level as they were growing in their original pots, and never bury the stems, which are prone to rotting in damp soil or potting mix. Once planted, add a ½–¾ in (1–2 cm) gravel mulch around the plants to prevent wet soil splashing up onto their leaves when it rains, which can also cause rotting.

Harvest the leaves of your herbs when they are growing well, usually from late spring to early fall, but never strip a plant completely, as they need their foliage to continue photosynthesizing and growing. Use sharp scissors to snip off sprigs as you need them, and stop harvesting when fall draws in and growth slows, even if you are growing evergreens such as bay or sage. Instead, dry leaves you have harvested earlier to use in winter— simply hang the stems upside down in a warm, dry place until the foliage is crisp.

**Plant herbs** such as chives at the same depth in the soil as they were growing in their original containers.

**TOP TIP** MINT SPREADS RAMPANTLY, SO GROW IT IN ITS OWN LARGE POT TO PREVENT IT SWAMPING YOUR BEDS AND BORDERS OR OTHER HERBS IN A MIXED CONTAINER.

# EASY-CARE HERBS

Herbs offer a great way to grow food for the kitchen without much effort. Perennial and shrubby types, such as those listed here, rarely suffer from pests or diseases when given the growing conditions they enjoy, and you can plant them in the ground or in pots. Once established, these herbs are drought-tolerant and they live for a number of years, delivering tasty leaves throughout the growing season from spring to early fall. Evergreen shrubs can provide a decorative feature in winter, too, offering interest when other herbs have died down.

## CHIVES *ALLIUM SCHOENOPRASUM*

**HEIGHT AND SPREAD** 12 × 12 in (30 × 30 cm)
**SOIL** Moist but well drained
**HARDINESS** Fully hardy
**SUN** ☼ ☼

A good choice for beginners, this perennial herb is a bulb, but it's usually either sown from seed or bought as a young plant in spring. Chives quickly form a clump of mild, onion-flavored leaves topped with edible, purple pompom flowers in summer. Ideal for growing in free-draining soil in the ground, this little herb can also be planted in a raised bed or pot, which would suit it best if you have wet clay soil. Grow enough chives to harvest them regularly from early summer to early fall without weakening the plants.

**Edible purple flowers** adorn chives' mildly onion-flavored stems in summer.

## BAY TREE *LAURUS NOBILIS*

**HEIGHT AND SPREAD** up to 40 × 30 ft (12 × 10 m)
**SOIL** Well drained
**HARDINESS** Hardy to 14°F (−10°C)
**SUN** ☼ ☼

Left to its own devices, bay will slowly grow into a large evergreen tree, but you can restrict its size by clipping it annually in early summer or growing it in a pot. The aromatic leaves are used to flavor savory dishes and can be picked from late spring to early fall—growth slows in winter, when you should refrain from harvesting. Bay is not fully hardy, and prefers a sheltered spot and free-draining soil, but it is very drought-tolerant and grows well in both shade and sun.

**Bay's leathery, aromatic** evergreen leaves create a year-round garden feature.

## MINT *MENTHA*

**HEIGHT AND SPREAD** up to 3 × 3 ft (1 × 1 m)
**SOIL** Moist but well drained
**HARDINESS** Fully hardy
**SUN** ☼ ☼

With a range of flavors to choose from, including garden mint (*Mentha spicata*), chocolate mint (*Mentha × piperita* f. *citrata* 'Chocolate'), and apple mint (*Mentha suaveolens*), this versatile herb offers something for everyone. However, a feature all mints share is their propensity to spread, and they will quickly fill a bed if left to roam free. The solution is to grow mint in a large container of potting mix, and water it twice a week in spring and summer. Setting it in some shade will reduce its watering needs.

**Pineapple mint** is the variegated form of apple mint, with pineapple-scented leaves.

## OREGANO *ORIGANUM VULGARE*

**HEIGHT AND SPREAD** 18 × 18 in (45 × 45 cm)
**SOIL** Well drained
**HARDINESS** Fully hardy
**SUN** ☼ ☀

Also known as wild marjoram, this spreading perennial has small, aromatic leaves and clusters of pink, bee-friendly flowers in summer and early fall. One of the easiest herbs to grow, it soon forms a clump of edible foliage and flowers, which can be harvested from late spring to late summer. It dislikes wet soil, so if you have heavy clay, grow it in a raised bed or pot filled with sandy potting mix. Remove small sprigs of leaves for the kitchen every week or two in order to encourage bushier growth.

**'Aureum'** has tasty golden leaves that color best when it is grown in full sun.

## ROSEMARY *SALVIA ROSMARINUS*

**HEIGHT AND SPREAD** up to 5 × 5 ft (1.5 × 1.5 m)
**SOIL** Well drained or moist but well drained
**HARDINESS** Hardy to 14°F (−10°C)
**SUN** ☼

Rosemary is a bushy evergreen shrub with needlelike dark green aromatic leaves and small violet-blue flowers in spring; more blooms often appear later in summer. Choose from the upright species or a trailing form, such as the Prostratus Group, that will cascade from the edge of a raised bed. Leaves can be harvested from early spring to fall—refrain from harvesting in winter when growth slows down or halts. It grows best in full sun and can be pruned lightly in spring to encourage bushier growth.

**An evergreen herb,** rosemary grows well in large containers of potting mix.

## SAGE *SALVIA OFFICINALIS*

**HEIGHT AND SPREAD** 20 × 20 in (50 × 50 cm)
**SOIL** Well drained or moist but well drained
**HARDINESS** Hardy to 5°F (−15°C)
**SUN** ☼ ☀

Sage is a decorative semi-evergreen shrub with gray-green aromatic leaves used in stuffings, herbal teas, soups, and casseroles. Colorful cultivars include 'Purpurascens', with its dark purple leaves, and 'Tricolor', which adds sparkling cream, pink, and green variegated foliage to an herb bed. Harvest the leaves from late spring until the lilac-blue flowers appear in summer. Sage is an undemanding plant, apart from its dislike of wet soil—grow it in a raised bed or pot if you have heavy clay.

**'Purpurascens'** is a beautiful dark purple cultivar with leaves that offer a distinctive sage flavor.

## COMMON THYME *THYMUS VULGARIS*

**HEIGHT AND SPREAD** 12 × 12 in (30 × 30 cm)
**SOIL** Well drained
**HARDINESS** Hardy to 5°F (−15°C)
**SUN** ☼ ☀

One of the most versatile herbs, thyme is a dwarf evergreen shrub with small, aromatic, gray-green leaves, and white or pink, bee-friendly, early summer flowers. Choose from the wide range of cultivars, such as the lemon-scented 'Doone Valley' for its citrus flavor, and 'Archers Gold', which will brighten up a bed with yellow foliage. Grow thyme in a raised bed or pot if you have heavy clay soil, and harvest it from late spring to midsummer, which will also encourage bushy growth.

**'Doone Valley'** is a variegated form of lemon thyme, featuring gold and green foliage and purple summer flowers.

# GROWING EASY-CARE SOFT FRUIT

By choosing soft fruit plants carefully, you can grow a range of delicious crops with the minimum of maintenance. Once established, these easy-to-grow plants will deliver their sweet fruits year after year if you prune them annually and mulch the soil with well-rotted compost or manure (*see p.59*) each spring or fall. Just follow these tips and turn to pp.72–73 for advice on choosing varieties and aftercare.

**The delicious sweet fruits** of fall raspberries continue to ripen until the first frosts before winter sets in.

## BLACKBERRIES

Wild blackberries are often considered weeds and have no trouble establishing themselves almost anywhere, while cultivated forms are better-behaved but still very easy to grow. Before planting blackberries, apply a mulch of well-rotted garden compost or manure in the fall. Buy plants in late winter or early spring, and dig a large hole that will accommodate the root ball easily. Check that the plants will be at the same level in the ground after planting as they were in their pots. If you have bought bare-root plants, look for the dark soil line on the stems, and bury them up to that point. When growing more than one blackberry, allow 8 ft (2.4 m) between plants. Immediately after planting, prune all the stems down to a bud about 9 in (23 cm) from the ground.

Blackberries produce long, arching stems that are best trained along sturdy horizontal wires attached to a wall or fence at 12 in (30 cm) intervals. Alternatively, stretch wires between stout, pressure-treated wooden posts 8 ft (2.4 m) long, hammering them 2 ft (60 cm) into the soil to secure them. Tie the stems onto the wires or fence posts with strong twine.

Water the plants regularly while they establish—a year after planting they will only need irrigating during long dry periods. Reapply a mulch each year, leaving a gap around the stems. Plants fruit on two-year-old stems and will generally not produce a crop of berries in the first year after a winter or spring planting. For pruning advice, see p.73.

**TOP TIP** TO PREVENT BIRDS FROM EATING YOUR BERRIES AND CURRANTS, COVER THE FRUITS WITH BIRD-PROOF NETTING BEFORE THEY RIPEN.

**Train the long, arching stems** of your blackberries along wires affixed to a fence or wall or stretched between sturdy posts.

# FALL RASPBERRIES

There are two types of raspberry: those that fruit in summer and varieties that produce a crop from midsummer to mid-fall. The former are quite fiddly to grow, as their stems need supporting and pruning is more complicated, so for the least amount of effort opt for fall fruits, which are much easier to maintain. Also known as Primocanes, the stems need no support, and plants produce small quantities of raspberries over a long period, rarely resulting in a glut.

Most fall raspberries are sold as bare-root plants in winter and should be planted as soon as they arrive, as long as the soil is not waterlogged or frozen. Soak the canes for 20 minutes if they appear dry. Dig a hole wider and a little deeper than the root ball. Plant the canes about 1 in (2.5 cm) deeper than they were growing in the nursery (look for the dark soil mark on the stems) and 24 in (60 cm) apart, with the same distance between rows. After planting, cut the canes down to 12 in (30 cm); new shoots will appear in spring and produce a crop in their first year. Water plants regularly until they are well established and apply a mulch of well-rotted garden compost or manure annually in spring. See p.73 for advice on pruning fall raspberries.

**Remove stick supports** and cut back your raspberry canes as soon as you have planted them.

**Fall raspberry plants** will produce reliable crops when grown in fertile soil and full sun or part shade.

# BLACK CURRANTS

Most black currants are sold as bare-root plants, which are available in winter, but you can also buy potted plants at other times of the year. Plant bare-roots as soon as they arrive, unless the soil is waterlogged or frozen; potted plants are best planted in spring. Avoid planting in sites prone to late spring frosts which may damage the flowers, resulting in fewer or no fruits later in the year.

Add a mulch of well-rotted garden compost or manure in the fall before planting. Water potted plants and soak bare-root plants in water for 20 minutes if they appear dry. Dig a planting hole large enough to accommodate the roots easily and plant the stems at the same level they were growing in their pots or, if bare-root, about 2 in (5 cm) lower than the soil mark on the stems. Space plants 5 ft (1.5 m) apart, with 5 ft (1.5 m) between rows. Immediately after planting, prune each shoot on bare-root plants to two or three healthy buds from the ground, which will encourage new stems to form in spring. Container-grown plants do not require initial pruning if planted in late spring or summer. Black currants will produce fruit on two-year-old stems, so they may not crop until their second year after planting. For pruning advice, see p.73.

**Look for black currant plants** that have some frost-resistance, as these will crop more reliably after a cold spring.

# EASY-TO-GROW FRUIT

Delicious home-grown fruits are a treat that everyone can enjoy, with many ideally suited to beginners looking for reliable edibles to grow in a small space. Those described here include hardy shrubs and trees that will survive low winter temperatures and a wide variety of soil conditions, as well as strawberries, which are perennial plants that produce fruit for a few years before they need replacing. All these tough plants require watering regularly until they are established and then just a little annual care to keep them healthy and fruiting.

## STRAWBERRY *FRAGARIA × ANANASSA*

**HEIGHT AND SPREAD** 12 × 18 in (30 × 45 cm)
**SOIL** Moist but well drained
**HARDINESS** Fully hardy
**SUN** ☼ ☀

Choose from summer-fruiting strawberries that crop in early or late summer; "everbearers," which produce their berries throughout summer and early fall; or shade-loving wild strawberries with sweet little fruits in summer and early fall. You can buy either bare root plants (runners) or potted plants in spring; plant into free-draining soil or peat-free potting mix in a pot or raised bed. Keep plants moist and apply a high-potash liquid feed every week or two after the flowers have faded.

**Summer-fruiting berries** crop best in their second and third years, then need replacing.

## BLACK CHOKEBERRY *ARONIA MELANOCARPA*

**HEIGHT AND SPREAD** up to 4 × 6 ft (1.2 × 2 m)
**SOIL** Moist but well drained
**HARDINESS** Fully hardy
**SUN** ☼ ☀

In late spring this North American shrub produces pollen-rich white flowers, similar to those of a hawthorn, followed in early fall by juicy black fruits, often called a superfood due to their high nutrient content. They are quite tart but make delicious compotes and jams when cooked. The foliage turns red in the fall, adding to this plant's decorative value. Once it is well established, chokeberry will grow almost unaided, although removing one in three of the older stems in winter will increase fruiting.

**White spring flowers** are followed by tart black berries in the fall.

## HONEYBERRY *LONICERA CAERULEA*

**HEIGHT AND SPREAD** up to 5 × 4 ft (1.5 × 1.2 m)
**SOIL** Moist but well drained
**HARDINESS** Fully hardy
**SUN** ☼

One of the easiest crops to grow, in summer honeyberry produces sweet fruits that taste like blueberries. This Asian native is very hardy and suffers from no pests or diseases, but buy at least two plants to allow cross-pollination needed for the fruits to form. Plant in spring in a bed mulched with well-rotted garden compost and water well until established. Honeyberries flower in late winter or early spring, which can be a problem in cold years when few insects are around to pollinate them.

**Remove some** of the older stems after fruiting in summer to encourage new shoots.

## PLUM TREE *PRUNUS DOMESTICA*

**HEIGHT AND SPREAD** up to 12 × 10 ft (4 × 3 m)
**SOIL** Moist but well drained
**HARDINESS** Fully hardy
**SUN** ☼ ☼

For a small space, choose a self-fertile plum tree grown on a dwarfing rootstock that limits its size. There are many eating varieties that will fit the bill, including the dark red 'Victoria', violet-blue 'Stanley', and yellow 'Mirabelle Golden Sphere'. All produce pink or white pollen-rich flowers in spring and the fruits in summer. To plant, follow the advice on p.41, and water during dry spells for the first three years. No pruning is needed, apart from the removal in summer of dead, diseased, or wayward stems.

**'Victoria'** is one of the most popular plum varieties, loved for its sweet, dark red fruits.

## BLACK CURRANT *RIBES NIGRUM*

**HEIGHT AND SPREAD** up to 5 × 5 ft (1.5 × 1.5 m)
**SOIL** Moist but well drained
**HARDINESS** Fully hardy
**SUN** ☼ ☼

Delicious in pies, jams, and cordials, the heavy-cropping, disease- and frost-resistant 'Ben Connan' and 'Ben Hope' are among the best varieties of black currant. Plant bushes from late fall to early spring, following the tips on p.71, and harvest the currants in bunches. Feed each spring with an all-purpose granular fertilizer. Three years after planting, prune the shrubs annually in late winter to boost fruiting, cutting a quarter to a third of the older black canes to the base (younger canes will be lighter in color).

**'Ben Connan'** is a disease-resistant variety with large, glossy, early summer fruits.

## BLACKBERRY *RUBUS FRUTICOSUS*

**HEIGHT AND SPREAD** 12 × 4 ft (4 × 1.2 m)
**SOIL** Moist but well drained
**HARDINESS** Fully hardy
**SUN** ☼ ☼

Blackberries crop reliably each year with very little aftercare. Buy a thornless cultivar, such as 'Loch Maree', 'Loch Ness', or 'Loch Tay', which will be easier to handle and to train along a wired wall or fence. Follow the planting and training advice on p.70. In fall, remove the old dark brown fruiting canes, leaving the green new shoots. Prune these stems to a healthy bud and cut back the side-stems to 12–16 in (30–40 cm) from the main stem. Feed with an all-purpose granular fertilizer in spring.

**'Loch Maree'** is a thornless cultivar that produces heavy crops of large, sweet fruits.

## FALL RASPBERRY *RUBUS IDAEUS*

**HEIGHT AND SPREAD** up to 5 × 2 ft (1.5 × 0.6 m)
**SOIL** Moist but well drained
**HARDINESS** Fully hardy
**SUN** ☼ ☼

Fall-fruiting varieties of raspberry crop from midsummer to early fall and are very easy to grow. Good disease-resistant varieties include the yellow-fruited 'All Gold' and traditional red 'Joan J', which produces large, juicy fruits. Follow the planting instructions on p.71 and water your raspberries regularly during dry periods, especially when the fruit is forming. To prune fall raspberries, simply cut all the canes down to the base in winter, and new fruiting stems will appear in spring.

**One of the best** fall-fruiting raspberries, 'Joan J' bears heavy crops of red fruits.

**Begonias** are very easy to grow in containers, requiring just one or two waterings a week to bear a profusion of beautiful blooms all summer.

# PLANTING IN CONTAINERS

Plants in containers generally require more attention than those in the ground, but there are some that are happier than others in the confines of a pot. Large vessels that hold more soil and water to sustain plants' roots will need watering less frequently than tiny containers, while drought-tolerant species are always good choices, whichever type of pot you choose. Covering the top of the potting mix will also help lock water inside a container, reducing the need to irrigate your plants as often.

# CHOOSING CONTAINERS AND POTTING MIXES

**Planting in pots is a great way to decorate patios and small paved spaces where there is no soil. More effort is required to keep plants healthy in containers because their roots cannot reach down into the water reservoirs found in the soil, so they rely on you to provide all their food and drink. However, you can reduce your workload by using simple techniques to retain moisture in the potting mix.**

**Larger containers** hold more potting mix and moisture and need watering less frequently than small pots.

## EASY-CARE CONTAINERS

When choosing containers for low-maintenance gardening, big is best, because large pots hold more potting mix and water and will sustain your plants unaided for longer. Reserve small pots for succulents such as houseleeks (*Sempervivum*) and sedums, which need only tiny amounts of moisture to survive. Whatever size or style of pot you choose, make sure it has drainage holes at the bottom to prevent waterlogging—wet, airless soil will soon cause rot, for which there is no cure.

Also consider the materials a pot is made from. Terra-cotta absorbs water and will draw moisture out of the potting mix, while dark-colored plastics and some metals heat up under hot sun, which will also dry out the contents of a pot. To avoid these problems, line the inside of your container with an insulating layer of recycled bubble wrap before planting. Also look for frost-proof guarantees when buying terra-cotta if you want your pots to survive cold winters intact.

When buying large pots, check that they will not be too heavy for you to move once filled with soil and plants, or decide on their final locations and fill them *in situ.*

**Wooden containers** are relatively light and a good choice for large plants such as clematis.

**Enriched potting mix** is ideal for fruit plants that will be in their containers for more than one season.

## CHOOSING POTTING MIXES

There are different types of potting mix to choose from, but a good rule of thumb is to use a peat-free mix for any plants that will be in a pot or hanging basket for a year or less, and a mix with added organic matter for those that will be in their containers over a longer period, such as trees, shrubs, and perennials. Enriched mix is a little heavier and will hold moisture better, too, so you could try a mix of both to sustain short-term potted plants in sunny sites. For plants that prefer acid soil, such as camellias and rhododendrons, choose an acidic mix to keep them happy.

Avoid any products containing peat, which is taken from peat bogs that support rare plants and wildlife and act as carbon sinks.

**TOP TIP** AN EASY AND EFFICIENT WAY TO REWET DRY POTTING MIX IS TO PLUNGE THE WHOLE PLANTED POT INTO A BUCKET OR TRAY OF WATER AND LEAVE IT UNTIL THE TOP LAYER GLISTENS WITH MOISTURE.

## MULCH FOR MOISTURE

Adding a layer of shredded bark, gravel, stone chips, recycled aggregates, or homemade compost over the mix in a pot will help to lock in moisture. This layer is known as a "mulch" and offers an easy way to reduce watering frequency and increase plant health. If using compost or bark, which are also water-absorbent, leave a space around the stems, especially those of trees and shrubs which may rot if in contact with these moist materials. For drought-loving flowers and herbs, use gravel, stone, or dry aggregates that will protect their stems and leaves from resting on wet soil and rotting.

**A gravel mulch** will both lock in moisture and keep the slender stems of plants such as species tulips dry.

## WATER IN RESERVE

Self-watering containers are a good option for time-poor gardeners. They have a built-in reservoir at the bottom, with an overflow outlet to prevent waterlogging and an indicator to show when it is empty. Most are made from plastic or recycled man-made materials, and while they may not look as elegant as a terra-cotta or stone pot, they are a practical choice for thirsty plants such as fruit and vegetables.

**Self-watering containers** cut watering times and are perfect for strawberries (*above*) and vegetables.

# PLANTING UP EASY-CARE POTS

The dry conditions in a pot mean that any plant with some drought-tolerance will be easier to care for than thirsty species that require lots of water to thrive. Plants that hail from arid areas are good choices and many feature special adaptations that help them survive dry periods. Other ideas include applying large doses of water when irrigating and installing automatic systems to reduce your workload.

**Shade-tolerant fuchsias** from South and Central America cope well with the dry conditions in a pot.

**Succulents have thick, fleshy leaves** that retain water and allow these plants to survive during droughts.

## CHOOSING PLANTS FOR CONTAINERS

Having selected a container that will hold sufficient water and nutrients to keep your plants happier for longer (*see p.76*), the next step is to choose some easy-care plants. Succulents, such as sedums, aloes, aeoniums, and houseleeks (*Sempervivum*), which have thick, fleshy leaves that act as water stores and allow them to survive dry periods, are good choices. These plants can survive for weeks without irrigation, even in a container, although offering them some water every fortnight will keep them in good health.

The sheen on silver-leaved plants, such as lavender and senecio, reflects the light, helping keep them cool and hydrated in a pot, and this adaptation means that they will need watering, and usually feeding, less frequently than plants adapted to thrive in moist soils. Plants from hot, dry climates such as Australia, Africa, South America, and the Mediterranean region also cope well in the dry conditions in a pot: kingfisher daisies (*Felicia*), pelargoniums, and Swan river daisies (*Brachyscome*), to name a few, fall into these groups. For more choices, see pp.80–89 and 92–95.

## PLANTING AND WATERING TIPS

Plant your container plants at the same depth as they were in their original pots, since burying the stems and leaves may cause them to rot. Also leave a gap of ¾–2 in (2–5 cm) between the top of the soil and the rim of the pot when the plants are in place. This will provide space for water to accumulate and seep down into the potting mix. Give plants a good soak at each watering— a larger dose every few days is better than a sprinkling every day, which will only penetrate the top of the soil and bring roots to the surface where they are more vulnerable. Use a hose on a gentle spray setting or a can with a rose head and aim the water at the potting mix, not the leaves or flowers. In summer, this may mean moving the foliage back to access the surface.

**Leave a space** between the potting mix and pot rim for water to accumulate.

## SITING YOUR POTS

Placing containers in some shade will lower evaporation rates and thereby also reduce the need to water them as frequently. Of course, some plants will not be happy in shade, so if you have sun-lovers set on a bright patio, try grouping them together. This trick will also help maintain thirsty plants, such as bedding lobelia. Plants expire moisture, just like we do, and they create their own moist micro-climate when placed close together. The overlapping leafy canopies will also help shield the top of the potting mix from the sun and prevent it from drying out quickly.

**Grouping plants** in pots together will create a moist micro-climate around them.

### NEED TO KNOW

- Use a potting mix that contains plant food to save you applying some when planting. After six weeks, add slow-release fertilizer granules, which should suffice for the rest of the growing season.
- To feed permanent plants in pots, in spring carefully scrape off some of the potting mix from the top and apply a slow-release granular fertilizer, together with some fresh mix.

## WATERING AIDS

There are many products on the market that cut pot maintenance. Automatic drip irrigation systems are a good choice if you don't have time to water your plants regularly. Most kits comprise a network of pipes attached to an automatic timer that fits onto an outdoor faucet, allowing you to program watering times. They can be a little fiddly to install and are quite expensive but do the job very well.

If you have just a few pots, you could try "ollas." Simply bury these unglazed, porous clay pots in the soil and fill with water. The moisture seeps through the clay, keeping the plant roots moist. Another option is a homemade wick and reservoir system: place a bucket or can of water above the level of your pots, dip one end of a strip of greenhouse capillary matting into the water and tuck the other end in the potting mix. The matting will keep the plants' roots moist for a week or two.

**Bury an olla** in small pots to help keep plant roots moist.

# EASY PLANTS FOR POTS

**When choosing plants for containers, you can opt for evergreen shrubs offering year-round color that only need watering and a little annual care, or, if you have more time, try flowering plants that bloom in different seasons to create an evolving display. Many plants for pots are annuals or bulbs that may need replanting every year, so assess your time constraints and select those that suit your needs best. You can also widen your choices with plants in the hanging basket section (see _pp.92–95_), which will be equally happy in a pot.**

## BELLIS DAISY _BELLIS PERENNIS_

**HEIGHT AND SPREAD** 6 × 6 in (15 × 15 cm)
**POTTING MIX** Peat-free
**HARDINESS** Fully hardy
**SUN** ☼ ☼

A cultivated form of the lawn daisy and equally hardy, these little plants make a beautiful display when the single or double pompom flowers appear in spring above spoon-shaped leaves. The flowers come in white, pink, and red. Plant these easy-to-grow evergreens in the fall along with spring bulbs to bloom the following year. In sheltered areas, bellis daisies may flower from late winter to early summer. In subsequent years, add an all-purpose granular fertilizer to plants in pots in early spring.

**The pompom** flowers of the Tasso Series will dress up pots from spring to early summer.

## BUGLE _AJUGA REPTANS_

**HEIGHT AND SPREAD** 6 × 12 in (15 × 30 cm)
**POTTING MIX** Peat-free enriched
**HARDINESS** Fully hardy
**SUN** ☼

Ideal for adding a leafy edge to a pot filled with daffodils or grape hyacinths, this spreading evergreen perennial also produces spikes of dark blue flowers in late spring and early summer. Look out for bugles with colorful foliage, such as the reddish-pink tinted 'Burgundy Glow' or dark purple-brown 'Catlin's Giant', which will provide color long after the flowers have faded. This plant will reflower each year if you add an all-purpose granular fertilizer in spring. Repot when it outgrows its home.

_Ajuga reptans_ **'Burgundy Glow'** produces colorful foliage and blue spring flowers.

## CAMELLIA _CAMELLIA_

**HEIGHT AND SPREAD** up to 6½ × 6½ ft (2 × 2 m) in a pot
**POTTING MIX** Acidic potting mix
**HARDINESS** Hardy to 5°F (−15°C)
**SUN** ☼ ☀

Loved for their large flowers, camellias are evergreen shrubs that thrive in pots. Choose from the fall- to winter-flowering _Camellia sasanqua_ or _C. japonica_ and _C. × williamsii_, which both flower in early spring. All require acidic potting mix and a sheltered position protected from early-morning sun, which can damage the blooms. Water weekly from spring to fall, and in early spring apply a slow-release feed for acid-loving plants. A bark mulch will also help lock moisture in the pot.

**The rose-pink flowers** of _Camellia_ × _williamsii_ 'Elsie Jury' appear in early spring.

# GRAPE HYACINTH *MUSCARI*

**HEIGHT AND SPREAD** 8 × 4 in (20 × 10 cm)
**POTTING MIX** Peat-free enriched
**HARDINESS** Fully hardy
**SUN** ☼ ☼

The grape hyacinth's spikes of small, blue or white, bell-shaped flowers make a colorful feature in a small pot of their own or in a larger container combined with other spring flowers. Plant the small bulbs in the fall to be rewarded with a glorious display the following spring. The pollen-rich blooms last for many weeks, and if you leave the bulbs in their pot they will pop up year after year—just use enriched potting mix and add a little all-purpose granular fertilizer in late winter.

**The blue flowers** of grape hyacinths perform over many weeks with just a weekly water.

# FORGET-ME-NOT *MYOSOTIS*

**HEIGHT AND SPREAD** 12 × 6 in (30 × 15 cm)
**POTTING MIX** Peat-free (any type)
**HARDINESS** Fully hardy
**SUN** ☼

The classic blue-flowered forget-me-nots that often self-seed among spring bulbs in a border also make a beautiful display of frothy blooms and spear-shaped foliage in a pot. Most species are biennial, producing leaves in their first year of growth and flowering in the second. Buy these drought-tolerant plants in spring for your pots. After the blooms are over, you may find seedlings which you can dig up in the fall and repot in fresh potting mix with some bulbs for flowers the following year.

**Forget-me-nots** produce masses of tiny blue flowers that combine well with daffodils.

# DAFFODIL *NARCISSUS*

**HEIGHT AND SPREAD** up to 18 × 12 in (45 × 30 cm)
**POTTING MIX** Peat-free (any type)
**HARDINESS** Fully hardy
**SUN** ☼ ☼

Harbingers of spring, daffodils are guaranteed to cheer up any patio pot with their sunny, trumpet-shaped blooms. Choose dwarf types such as 'Tête-à-tête', 'Minnow', and 'Elka' for small containers or taller varieties for larger pots. Plant the bulbs in the fall for blooms the following spring. After flowering, you can compost the plants, or pinch off the faded blooms and apply a high-potash fertilizer to the pot every two weeks until the foliage turns yellow. Then leave them *in situ* or plant the bulbs in a border.

**Flowers in shades** of pale lemon make 'Elka' a good choice for a mixed pot display.

# TULIP *TULIPA*

**HEIGHT AND SPREAD** up to 24 × 10 in (60 × 20 cm)
**POTTING MIX** Peat-free
**HARDINESS** Fully hardy
**SUN** ☼ ☼

The sheer wealth of colors, flower shapes, and sizes make tulips among the most popular of all spring container plants. Plant the bulbs in the fall for a display the following year—cover pots with chicken wire weighted down with a stone to deter squirrels, then remove it when the shoots appear. Tulips tend to flower best in a pot of their own, and although the standard advice is to grow them in full sun, these bulbs will thrive in a little shade, too. Treat them as annuals, as few will reflower the following year.

**'Abu Hassan'** will brighten up a spring pot with its tall stems of gold-edged red flowers.

# AEONIUM *AEONIUM*

**HEIGHT AND SPREAD** up to 24 × 24 in (60 × 60 cm)
**POTTING MIX** Peat-free enriched, with added sand
**HARDINESS** Hardy to 41°F (5°C)
**SUN** ☼ ☼

Drought-tolerant and easy to grow, aeoniums are evergreen succulents that double as houseplants in winter and outdoor potted plants in summer. The most popular are cultivars of *Aeonium arboreum*, which produce a treelike silhouette with woody stems terminating in leafy rosettes. Sprays of small, cream or yellow flowers may appear in late spring. After the frosts, set plants outside in a bright, sheltered spot, shaded at midday. Water weekly and apply a balanced liquid fertilizer 2–3 times during the summer.

**The dark purple-leaved** *Aeonium* 'Zwartkop' has a branching, treelike shape.

# AFRICAN LILY *AGAPANTHUS*

**HEIGHT AND SPREAD** up to 36 × 20 in (90 × 50 cm)
**POTTING MIX** Peat-free enriched
**HARDINESS** Hardy from 34–23°F (1°C to −5°C)
**SUN** ☼

These elegant South African perennials make a statement in large pots on a sunny patio, with their strappy leaves and their stems of spherical flower heads in shades of blue, purple, and white which appear from late summer. Deciduous types are the hardiest and will survive a mild winter outside in a sheltered area close to the house—bring others into a frost-free garage or cool room indoors. Water once a week, and apply a seaweed feed fortnightly from spring until the flowers open.

*Agapanthus* **'Northern Star'** is a hardy cultivar that will survive a mild winter outside.

# SNAPDRAGON *ANTIRRHINUM*

**HEIGHT AND SPREAD** 20 × 12 in (50 × 30 cm)
**POTTING MIX** Peat-free
**HARDINESS** Hardy to 23°F (−5°C)
**SUN** ☼

Loved for their unusual flowers, which resemble dragons' mouths when gently pinched, these annuals make a colorful display throughout summer. The blooms come in all shades of white, yellow, orange, pink, and red. Use the tall types as a focal point in a large pot or try dwarf hybrids in window boxes. As they are drought-tolerant, snapdragons need watering only once or twice a week. Some may overwinter in a pot on a sheltered patio. Remove faded flower heads to prolong the display.

**The Liberty Classic Series** comes in a choice of yellows, oranges, pinks, and reds.

# BACOPA *CHAENOSTOMA CORDATUM*

**HEIGHT AND SPREAD** 4 × 12 in (10 × 30 cm)
**POTTING MIX** Peat-free
**HARDINESS** Hardy to 34°F (1°C)
**SUN** ☼

Softening the edge of a summer container with its trailing stems of small green leaves and white, pink, blue, or mauve little flowers, bacopa makes a great match for upright container plants in complementary colors. This annual plant demands full sun, but apart from that, it is easy to maintain. Plant out after the frosts, water twice a week and apply a high-potash fertilizer every fortnight from midsummer. Bacopa does not require deadheading, but removing straggly stems will keep it looking neat.

**White-flowered bacopa** tends to bloom more profusely in a pot than other colors.

## SWAN RIVER DAISY *BRACHYSCOME IBERIDIFOLIA*

**HEIGHT AND SPREAD** 10 × 10 in (25 × 25 cm)
**POTTING MIX** Peat-free
**HARDINESS** Hardy to 34°F (1°C)
**SUN** ☼

This diminutive annual daisy combines soft, ferny foliage with a carpet of starry flowers, and works well as an edging plant in larger containers with taller plants such as pelargoniums. It is drought-tolerant and will sail through hot summers unscathed, even in small pots. Plant it out after the frosts in a sunny spot—it will cope with some shade each day but flowering may be reduced—and water twice a week. Deadhead occasionally and revitalize older plants by snipping off the faded stems.

**Swan river daisies** create a cushion of color with their small, yellow-centered flowers.

## POT MARIGOLD *CALENDULA OFFICINALIS*

**HEIGHT AND SPREAD** up to 24 × 12 in (60 × 30 cm)
**POTTING MIX** Peat-free
**HARDINESS** Hardy to 5°F (−15°C)
**SUN** ☼ ◑

Hardy and relatively free of problems, pot marigolds were traditionally grown in containers, hence their common name, and are still a favorite for patio displays today. These annuals are drought-resistant and need watering just once or twice a week in summer. They bloom over a long period, flowering up to the first frosts in the fall. Deadhead them now and again to sustain the show, but leave a few faded flowers intact to self-seed in the garden and provide free plants for the following year.

**Single-flowered marigolds** offer bright colors and rich stores of pollen for bees.

## COSMOS *COSMOS*

**HEIGHT AND SPREAD** up to 36 × 18 in (90 × 45 cm)
**POTTING MIX** Peat-free multipurpose
**HARDINESS** Hardy to 23°F (−5°C)
**SUN** ☼

The ferny foliage and large flowers of the tender annual *Cosmos bipinnatus* make it a good candidate for a summer pot, while the slightly hardier perennial *C. atrosanguineus* 'Chocolate' offers unusual, chocolate-scented, dark red blooms. Mature plants are easy to grow, but young cosmos can fall prey to slugs and snails, so keep them indoors until they are well established before planting out after the frosts. Water twice a week and feed with a high-potash fertilizer in late summer to sustain flowering.

***Cosmos bipinnatus*** produces large, showy flowers in summer but dies when the frosts arrive.

## PINEAPPLE LILY *EUCOMIS BICOLOR*

**HEIGHT AND SPREAD** 24 × 12 in (60 × 30 cm)
**POTTING MIX** Peat-free enriched, with added sand
**HARDINESS** Hardy to 14°F (−10°C)
**SUN** ☼

This bulb commands attention on a patio when its spectacular pineapple-like flowers appear in summer. The blooms comprise small, purple-edged, pale green flowers topped with a leafy rosette. Despite their exotic appearance, these plants can survive winter on a sheltered patio if the soil is dry. To achieve this, turn the container on its side in the fall after the leaves have died down, or bring it indoors in cold areas. Plant the bulbs in spring and water twice a week; apply an all-purpose granular feed each spring.

**Exotic-looking** pineapple lilies are quite hardy if their soil is kept dry in winter.

## TREASURE FLOWER *GAZANIA*

**HEIGHT AND SPREAD** up to 12 × 12 in (30 × 30 cm)
**POTTING MIX** Peat-free
**HARDINESS** Hardy to 34°F (1°C)
**SUN** ☼

The treasure flower is aptly named; its colorful jewel-like blooms and silver-gray leaves take center stage in a pot on a sunny patio. The plants make a dazzling display when grown on their own or with other flowers that like similar conditions. Demanding little attention, these South African beauties need watering about once a week in summer, but sun is essential, as the flowers will close in shade or dull weather. Plant out after the frosts, feed monthly with a high-potash fertilizer, and deadhead for a longer show.

**The large, striped blooms** make *Gazania* 'New Day Rose Stripe' a popular potted plant.

## JAPANESE FOREST GRASS *HAKONECHLOA MACRA*

**HEIGHT AND SPREAD** 14 × 16 in (35 × 40 cm)
**POTTING MIX** Peat-free enriched
**HARDINESS** Fully hardy
**SUN** ☼ ☼ ☼ ☼

This gently cascading grass makes a beautiful feature in a medium-size to large pot. The bright green leaves are joined by sprays of lime-green flowers from midsummer, and the foliage develops reddish-brown tints in the fall; it may persist into winter in milder areas. After planting, apply a mulch of rotted compost or manure to retain moisture, and water the plant twice a week in the growing season. In early spring, remove dead foliage, feed with an all-purpose granular fertilizer and renew the mulch.

**Golden Japanese forest grass** (*H. macra* 'Aureola') has bright yellow and green foliage.

## SHRUBBY VERONICA *HEBE*

**HEIGHT AND SPREAD** up to 36 × 36 in (90 × 90 cm) in a pot
**POTTING MIX** Peat-free enriched
**HARDINESS** Hardy to 14°F (−10°C)
**SUN** ☼ ☼

Shrubby veronicas are evergreen shrubs that provide year-round foliage interest, while their pollen-rich white, pink, purple, or blue flowers offer colorful accents in summer. Choose a compact type for a pot; if you live in a cold area, select one of the varieties with small green leaves, which are the hardiest types. Water these New Zealand natives about once a week in the growing season, and in spring apply an all-purpose granular feed. Move tender hebes into a frost-free place over winter.

**Hebe 'Silver Queen'** sports bright, variegated foliage and purple summer flowers.

## HYDRANGEA *HYDRANGEA MACROPHYLLA*

**HEIGHT AND SPREAD** up to 4 × 4 ft (1.2 × 1.2 m) in a pot
**POTTING MIX** Peat-free enriched
**HARDINESS** Hardy to 5°F (−15°C)
**SUN** ☼

Hydrangeas are deciduous shrubs that make long-lasting container plants; their showy, rounded or slightly flattened flower heads provide color throughout summer, with pretty seed heads then adding to the show. Select a compact cultivar and grow it in a large pot with space for the roots to expand. Water twice a week in the growing season. In spring, apply an all-purpose granular fertilizer (for blue-flowered varieties, use one for acid-lovers), and cut the stems down to a healthy bud, while removing any dead growth.

**Hydrangea macrophylla** 'Lanarth White' is a lacecap type with white and pink blooms.

## LAVENDER *LAVANDULA*

**HEIGHT AND SPREAD** up to 32 × 24 in (80 × 60 cm)
**POTTING MIX** Peat-free enriched
**HARDINESS** Hardy to 5°F (−15°C)
**SUN** ☼

English lavender (*Lavandula angustifolia*) and the French form (*L. stoechas*) provide year-round color with their aromatic silvery evergreen foliage and spikes of fragrant blue, pink, or white summer flowers. French lavender comes into bloom earlier, from late spring, but it's not as hardy. In spring, apply an all-purpose granular fertilizer, and water plants once a week in the growing season. Remove the flower spikes after blooming and in spring cut English lavender stems down to a healthy bud.

**French lavender** features distinctive long petallike bracts on top of each flower.

## TENDER GERANIUM *PELARGONIUM*

**HEIGHT AND SPREAD** 20 × 12 in (50 × 30 cm)
**POTTING MIX** Peat-free
**HARDINESS** Hardy to 41°F (5°C)
**SUN** ☼ ☼

Perfect for brightening up a patio, tender geraniums are among the easiest plants to grow in a container. Plant a trailing type at a pot edge; for the center, choose one with scented leaves or an upright form, which include shrubby Regal varieties, compact Angel types, and Zonal pelargoniums that feature a dark band on the leaves. Very drought-tolerant, these perennials need just a weekly watering and an occasional dose of high-potash fertilizer. You can overwinter plants on a windowsill indoors.

*Pelargonium* **'Margaret Soley'** is a Regal form with rich pink-edged red flowers.

## FAN FLOWER *SCAEVOLA AEMULA*

**HEIGHT AND SPREAD** 12 × 24 in (30 × 60 cm)
**POTTING MIX** Peat-free
**HARDINESS** Hardy to 41°F (5°C)
**SUN** ☼

An Australian native, this tender annual has unusual fan-shaped blue summer flowers, which appear over tooth-edged leaves. Its trailing habit makes it a good edging plant for a container filled with complementary brightly colored upright flowers. It grows best in full sun but will tolerate shade for a few hours a day. The fleshy leaves protect it from drought— a weekly water is all it needs when grown in a pot. It will also benefit from a high-potash fertilizer every 2–3 weeks from midsummer.

**The unusual** fan flower is very drought-tolerant and makes an intriguing edging plant.

## COLEUS *SOLENOSTEMON*

**HEIGHT AND SPREAD** 12 × 12 in (30 × 30 cm)
**POTTING MIX** Peat-free
**HARDINESS** Hardy to 41°F (5°C)
**SUN** ☼ ☼

Grown for its lobed foliage, coleus adds long-lasting color to a summer container display. The leaves come in a wide range of colors, from lime greens to pinks, purples, oranges, and reds, while spikes of tiny tubular flowers add yet more color when they appear in summer. Plant this perennial outside after the frosts and water it about twice a week. Remove faded flowering stems to keep the plant neat, and bring it indoors before temperatures dive in the fall if you want to keep it for the following year.

*Solenostemon* **'Pink Devil'** produces frilly-edged pink, purple, and green leaves.

## SEDGE *CAREX*

**HEIGHT AND SPREAD** up to 32 × 32 in (80 × 80 cm)
**POTTING MIX** Peat-free enriched
**HARDINESS** Fully hardy
**SUN** ☼ ☼ ☀

Evergreen sedges produce graceful fountains of grasslike foliage that add impact to a fall or winter container display. The best types for pots include the metallic-colored *Carex comans* bronze-leaved; golden *C. elata* 'Aurea'; striped *C. oshimensis* 'Evergold'; and shade-tolerant *C.* 'Ice Dance'. Water them during dry spells in the fall and they will then take care of themselves through winter. In spring, remove dead leaves and apply an all-purpose granular fertilizer. Water weekly in spring and summer.

**The striped leaves** of *Carex* 'Ice Dance' make a striking feature in a winter container.

## DWARF JAPANESE CEDAR *CRYPTOMERIA JAPONICA*

**HEIGHT AND SPREAD** up to 36 × 36 in (90 × 90 cm)
**POTTING MIX** Peat-free enriched
**HARDINESS** Fully hardy
**SUN** ☼ ☼

Check labels carefully when buying a Japanese cedar, as the species will grow into a large tree. However, dwarf cultivars such as 'Globosa Nana' and 'Golden Promise' make beautiful winter potted plants, forming neat domes of dark or yellow-green textured foliage. 'Golden Promise' also has purple tints in winter. Provide shelter from strong winds, which can damage the foliage, and water these conifers weekly from spring to early fall. Feed in spring with an all-purpose granular fertilizer.

**Compact** *Cryptomeria japonica* 'Globosa Nana' forms a dense dome of evergreen foliage.

## EASTERN CYCLAMEN *CYCLAMEN COUM*

**HEIGHT AND SPREAD** 4 × 6 in (10 × 15 cm)
**POTTING MIX** Peat-free enriched
**HARDINESS** Hardy to 5°F (−15°C)
**SUN** ☼

While some larger-flowered cyclamen are not hardy, this little beauty weathers cold temperatures and will provide late winter color in a pot when the dainty blooms appear. The rounded, often marbled foliage also offers interest earlier in the season before the pink or white flowers open. In the fall, plant it in a container of its own or with ferns, and water regularly. Add a leaf mold mulch in spring as the leaves fade. This perennial tuber dies down in summer, when it can survive long, dry periods.

**Eastern cyclamen's** small pink flowers over silver and green leaves liven up a pot.

## WINTER HEATH *ERICA CARNEA*

**HEIGHT AND SPREAD** up to 8 × 18 in (20 × 45 cm)
**POTTING MIX** Peat-free enriched, preferably acidic
**HARDINESS** Fully hardy
**SUN** ☼ ☼

Not to be confused with heather (*Calluna vulgaris*), which flowers from midsummer, heaths generally bloom from winter to early spring. The small, urn-shaped flowers come in shades of pink or white and appear over needlelike evergreen leaves. Largely pest- and disease-free, this little shrub prefers acidic potting mix, but will nevertheless do well in any enriched product. Trim old stems after flowering, apply an all-purpose granular fertilizer in spring, and water regularly during dry periods.

**'Springwood White'** produces trailing mats of bright green foliage and white flowers.

## JAPANESE ARALIA *FATSIA JAPONICA*

**HEIGHT AND SPREAD** 4 × 4 ft (1.2 × 1.2 m)
**POTTING MIX** Peat-free enriched
**HARDINESS** Hardy to 5°F (−15°C)
**SUN** ☀ ☀ ☀

The large lobed leaves of Japanese aralia create a sculptural focal point on a patio all year. In the fall, it also bears white spherical flower heads, loved by bees and other pollinators, followed by small black winter berries. Despite its tropical appearance, this tough shrub is hardy and survives periods of drought—a weekly water in summer is all it requires if grown in some shade; water it more frequently in sun. Remove old leaves as they fade and apply an all-purpose granular feed each spring.

**Choose a large pot** for this Japanese evergreen to create a dramatic year-round display.

## SNOWDROP *GALANTHUS*

**HEIGHT AND SPREAD** up to 8 × 4 in (20 × 10 cm)
**POTTING MIX** Peat-free enriched
**HARDINESS** Hardy to 5°F (−15°C)
**SUN** ☀ ☀

These classic white winter flowers are longstanding favorites and there are hundreds of varieties to choose from, some with double flowers, others sporting elegant green markings. All look lovely in pots when the dainty blooms open in late winter. Plant them while in bud or flower and water regularly until the blooms fade. To provide these bulbs with the moisture they need, even when dormant, plant them in a shady border; you can dig them up as shoots appear in winter and repot.

**'Cowhouse Green'** is a tall snowdrop with elegant green striped markings.

## CHRISTMAS ROSE *HELLEBORUS NIGER*

**HEIGHT AND SPREAD** 12 × 12 in (30 × 30 cm)
**POTTING MIX** Peat-free enriched
**HARDINESS** Fully hardy
**SUN** ☀

The Christmas rose flowers earlier than many hellebores; its clear white or pink-flushed, bowl-shaped blooms open in midwinter. The lobed foliage also overwinters—just remove the old leaves in late winter or early spring to make way for new growth and prevent the disease leaf spot occurring. Grow it in a pot of its own or in a large container with other winter plants, and keep the potting mix moist. Apply a mulch of well-rotted compost or manure each fall and feed in spring with an all-purpose granular fertilizer.

**The clear white** blooms of the Christmas rose make a beautiful display in a winter pot.

## FOAMY BELLS × *HEUCHERELLA*

**HEIGHT AND SPREAD** 18 × 8 in (45 × 20 cm)
**POTTING MIX** Peat-free enriched
**HARDINESS** Fully hardy
**SUN** ☀

This plant is a marriage between *Heuchera*, with its colorful lobed foliage, and the slightly tougher but less showy *Tiarella*. The result is a semi-evergreen perennial with good disease resistance that makes a beautiful winter potted plant. Leaf colors range from lime green and gold to orange, red, and purple. Tiny flowers add to the show in late spring. Make sure the potting mix doesn't dry out in winter, and water twice a week in the growing season. Add an all-purpose granular fertilizer and a mulch in spring.

**'Tapestry'** has unusual lobed green and purple leaves that will endure in a sheltered spot.

## SWITCH IVY *LEUCOTHOE*

**HEIGHT AND SPREAD** up to 36 × 36 in (90 × 90 cm) in a pot
**POTTING MIX** Acidic
**HARDINESS** Fully hardy
**SUN** ☼ ☀

Also known as dog hobble, *Leucothoe* is a tough, hardy, evergreen shrub with decorative foliage that often changes color as the year progresses. The popular SCARLETTA, for example, has maroon young foliage that turns green as it matures, and then takes on bronze tints in the fall and winter. Sprays of white spring flowers are a bonus. Switch ivy is easy to grow, only demanding moist, acidic potting mix to thrive. Add a fertilizer for acid-loving plants in spring and cover the potting mix with a mulch.

**SCARLETTA** produces glossy maroon and green leaves that take on bronze tints in the fall.

## CREEPING JENNY *LYSIMACHIA NUMMULARIA*

**HEIGHT AND SPREAD** 4 × 24 in (10 × 60 cm)
**POTTING MIX** Peat-free enriched
**HARDINESS** Hardy to 5°F (−15°C)
**SUN** ☼ ☀

This evergreen perennial is often used as ground cover, but its trailing stems of small green or golden leaves also make a decorative edge for a pot; small yellow flowers appear in summer, too. Best grown with taller evergreen shrubs or perennials for a lively display, it rarely suffers from pests or diseases and will soldier on in all weathers. Water it during long dry spells in winter, and then more consistently throughout the growing season. Apply an all-purpose granular fertilizer and a mulch in spring.

**The cultivar 'Aurea'** (golden creeping Jenny) makes a frill of bright foliage for a pot edge.

## NEW ZEALAND FLAX *PHORMIUM*

**HEIGHT AND SPREAD** up to 36 × 36 in (90 × 90 cm)
**POTTING MIX** Peat-free enriched, with added sand
**HARDINESS** Hardy to 14°F (−10°C)
**SUN** ☼ ☀

With its fountain of colorful, sword-shaped leaves, this evergreen perennial creates a dramatic focal point in a large pot in fall and winter. It is not fully hardy, but will survive in milder regions in a container. Plant it in a sheltered area out of cold winds and water once or twice a week from spring to fall. In spring, remove old or dead foliage and apply an all-purpose granular fertilizer. The cabbage palm *Cordyline australis* looks similar but is not as hardy.

**Phormiums** come in a wide array of foliage colors and variegations, including pinks and dark purples.

## WHITE SPRUCE *PICEA GLAUCA* DWARF SPECIES

**HEIGHT AND SPREAD** up to 4 × 4 ft (1.2 × 1.2 m) in a pot
**POTTING MIX** Acidic
**HARDINESS** Fully hardy
**SUN** ☼

While the species *Picea glauca* will grow into a large tree, dwarf forms, such as *P. glauca* var. *albertiana* 'Conica' and the blue-leaved *P. pungens* (Glauca Group) 'Hoopsii', are perfect for large pots; their colorful evergreen foliage provides interest through the colder months. Set these conifers in a sheltered spot and water during dry spells in winter but more frequently throughout the growing season. They need no pruning—just apply a fertilizer for acid-loving plants each spring and add a bark mulch.

**The evergreen** foliage of a dwarf white spruce creates a colorful focal point on a patio.

## PITTOSPORUM *PITTOSPORUM TENUIFOLIUM*

**HEIGHT AND SPREAD** up to 36 × 24 in (90 × 60 cm)
**POTTING MIX** Peat-free enriched
**HARDINESS** Hardy to 14°F (−10°C)
**SUN** ☼ ☼

Pittosporums are evergreen shrubs and the most commonly available species, *Pittosporum tenuifolium*, will grow into a large plant, but compact cultivars are suitable for pots. A popular choice is the aptly named 'Tom Thumb', which has wavy-edged, dark purple leaves that are green when young, creating an eye-catching two-tone effect in spring. Plant it in a sheltered area out of drying winds and water once or twice a week in the growing season. In spring, apply an all-purpose granular fertilizer and a mulch.

**'Tom Thumb'** is a dwarf cultivar with dark purple leaves in fall and winter.

## POLYPODY *POLYPODIUM*

**HEIGHT AND SPREAD** 12 × 24 in (30 × 60 cm)
**POTTING MIX** Peat-free enriched
**HARDINESS** Fully hardy
**SUN** ☼

Polypody is a shade-loving evergreen fern with finely divided leaves, known as fronds, that form a fountain of color in a pot all year. Most species and cultivars are compact and easy to grow. Tolerant of drought, they need watering a couple times a week from spring to early fall when grown in part shade, and should take care of themselves in winter—water them only if the weather is exceptionally dry. Feed these ferns in spring with an all-purpose granular fertilizer and apply a mulch.

**Polypodium glycyrrhiza 'Longicaudatum'** forms textured arching fronds.

## HOUSELEEK *SEMPERVIVUM*

**HEIGHT AND SPREAD** 4 × 4 in (10 × 10 cm)
**POTTING MIX** 50:50 peat-free enriched and sand
**HARDINESS** Fully hardy
**SUN** ☼

Perfect for an alpine trough or small pot, these diminutive succulents put on a year-round show with rosettes of colorful evergreen leaves. They are available in shades of red, purple, and green; the popular cobweb species (*Sempervivum arachnoideum*) also sports an unusual downy leaf covering. Starry flowers push out from the center of the leaf rosettes in summer. Among the easiest plants to grow in pots, they just need protection from excessive rain in winter and fortnightly watering in the growing season.

**Place pots** of houseleeks on an outdoor table to admire their intricate textured foliage.

## JAPANESE SKIMMIA *SKIMMIA JAPONICA*

**HEIGHT AND SPREAD** up to 36 × 36 in (90 × 90 cm) in a pot
**POTTING MIX** Acidic
**HARDINESS** Hardy to 5°F (−15°C)
**SUN** ☼ ☼

This evergreen shrub is a must for a cold-season container display. Its dark green, leathery leaves are joined in winter by either white- or red-budded flower heads on male plants or bright red berries on females. Grow both a male and female plant together if you want berries. White flowers, scented on female varieties, follow in spring. Plant skimmias in acidic potting mix and water once or twice a week in the growing season. Add a fertilizer for acid-loving plants each spring.

**'Rubella'** is a male form that produces red flower buds in winter over the glossy leaves.

# PLANTING A LOW-MAINTENANCE BASKET

Plants grown in hanging baskets make beautiful features, but they can be time-consuming to maintain. Most are compact in size, holding small quantities of potting mix and water to sustain the plants inside, and open-sided wire baskets that also allow water to drain through rapidly may require watering every day. However, if you want a few baskets, there are some easy ways to reduce the workload.

To reduce the care needed for baskets, install an automatic watering system.

## BASKET TYPES AND SITES

Baskets made from lightweight materials such as rattan or metal wire are popular, but those with solid sides and a plastic lining will usually offer better insulation and retain moisture longer. Alternatively, try making a basket from an upcycled colander, old shopping bag, or any durable vessel that offers drainage and is not too heavy to hang up. Avoid tiny baskets, which will dry out very quickly and require lots of care. Remember, too, that a basket hanging in full sun will need watering more frequently than one located in semi-shade.

## LINING OPTIONS

All plant containers need drainage, and hanging baskets are no exception. If you buy one with a plastic liner, snip a few holes around the sides 1 in (2.5 cm) from the base to create a shallow reservoir. This will help retain water and keep the potting mix moist, while allowing any excess to drain out. Baskets lined with coir will drain automatically since this is a naturally porous material, but they can lose water too quickly, so create a reservoir by lining the base with plastic cut from an old bag. Lining all free-draining baskets in this way will reduce their watering needs.

## WATERING TIPS

The primary task needed to maintain all hanging baskets is watering. Use a fine spray on a hose or a rose head attached to a watering can and target the potting mix rather than the flowers or leaves. This will ensure that the moisture reaches the roots, where it is needed. Purchase a watering wand that enables you to water at or above head-height, or retractable pulley systems that allow you to lower your baskets to water them more easily. If you have a few baskets to irrigate and no time to water them by hand, attach drip hoses connected to an automatic watering system (see pp.130–131).

Transform a shopping bag into a plant basket by lining it with recycled plastic.

Create a shallow reservoir at the base of a coir-lined basket with an old plastic bag.

## POTTING MIX AND MULCH

When planting up a summer basket, choose a potting mix that contains enough nutrients to support your plants for a few weeks. You can then add a slow-release fertilizer to keep them healthy for the rest of the season. Fall and winter baskets will not need a top-up of fertilizer until spring, since plants grow slowly or not at all during the colder months. Also add a ¾-in (2-cm) layer of gravel, aggregates, or fine bark chips over the potting mix to reduce evaporation and lock in moisture.

**Crushed seashells,** a waste product from the shellfish industry, make an excellent mulch for hanging baskets.

## CREATING AN EASY-CARE BASKET

**YOU WILL NEED** Large rattan basket • Scissors • Potting mix • Hose or watering can • Easy-care ornamental plants or herbs (see *pp.92–95 and pp.68–69*) • Bracket or wire for hanging

1 Snip drainage holes in the plastic liner 1 in (2.5 cm) from the base of the basket. If your basket has no liner, use an old plastic bag to line it (see *opposite*). Fill the basket to about 2 in (5 cm) below the rim.

2 Water the plants well, then plant them at the same level in the potting mix as they were in their pots. Fill in around the plants with potting mix, making sure that there is a gap of 1 in (2.5 cm) between the surface and rim of the basket to allow space for watering.

3 Press the potting mix down gently to remove any large air gaps and water well.

4 Either screw a metal hanging-basket bracket to a wall or fence post, or use sturdy wire wound around a roof beam of a pergola or arch from which to hang your basket. Water the basket twice a week, or three times during a hot summer.

# EASY-CARE BASKET PLANTS

Choosing the right plants for your hanging baskets will greatly reduce the effort needed to keep your displays looking their best. This selection of drought-resistant types will help keep watering to a minimum, and you can lower your basket's maintenance requirements further by opting for shade-tolerant plants and placing them in a cool area, where evaporation rates are lower. These plants are not greedy feeders and will thrive on the nutrients in the potting mix for a few weeks, after which you can add a slow-release fertilizer.

## BEGONIA *BEGONIA*

**HEIGHT AND SPREAD** up to 12 × 12 in (30 × 30 cm)
**POTTING MIX** Peat-free
**HARDINESS** Hardy to 34°F (1°C)
**SUN** ☀

There are hundreds of different begonias to choose from, since these shade- and drought-tolerant plants come in a wide range of colors and flower shapes. For baskets, try the trailing types, such as those in the Starshine and Illumination Series, with their dragon-wing-shaped leaves and small, pendulous flowers. No deadheading is needed for continuous blooms from summer to fall. Plant after the frosts in a cool area that receives a few hours of sun each day and water a couple of times a week.

*Begonia* **'Starshine Series'** produces cascading stems of colorful pendent flowers.

## MILLION BELLS *CALIBRACHOA*

**HEIGHT AND SPREAD** 6 × 12 in (15 × 30 cm)
**POTTING MIX** Peat-free
**HARDINESS** Hardy to 34°F (1°C)
**SUN** ☀

Resembling tiny petunias, these compact plants put on a colorful show from summer to fall, when their stems tumble from a basket, creating a waterfall of flowers. The blooms come in a huge range of colors, from fiery reds and oranges to cool blues and pale yellow. They also flower continuously without the need for any deadheading. Plant them outside after the frosts and water twice a week for the best results. Cut back any straggly stems later in the season to rejuvenate plants.

**The small, colorful flowers** of calibrachoas produce an eye-catching display in a basket.

## SPIDER PLANT *CHLOROPHYTUM COMOSUM*

**HEIGHT AND SPREAD** 12 × 12 in (30 × 30 cm)
**POTTING MIX** Peat-free
**HARDINESS** Hardy to 34°F (1°C)
**SUN** ☀

More commonly grown as an easy-care houseplant, the spider plant's almost indestructible qualities also make it an excellent choice for a summer basket outside. Sailing through periods of drought and happy in shade, this striped beauty makes the perfect partner for begonias and fuchsias. The baby plantlets that dance on long, curved stems add to its charms. Plant it after the frosts but bring the basket inside when temperatures drop again in the fall. Water once or twice a week.

**The spider plant's** striped foliage makes a good foil for bright, shade-tolerant flowers.

## DIASCIA *DIASCIA*

**HEIGHT AND SPREAD** 12 × 12 in (30 × 30 cm)
**POTTING MIX** Peat-free
**HARDINESS** Hardy to 23°F (−5°C)
**SUN** ☼

These South African plants cope well with drought and are perfect for baskets from summer to late fall when their wiry stems are covered with dainty flowers. Colors range from pink and apricot to red and white. Plants do not need deadheading, although trimming the stems occasionally will renew their vigor. Plant them outside after the frosts and water twice a week during summer. They tolerate temperatures just below freezing and may revive after a mild winter to bloom the following year.

*Diascia* **'Joyce's Choice'** has pale salmon flowers that team up well with purple blooms.

## SILVER LACE VINE *DICHONDRA ARGENTEA*

**HEIGHT AND SPREAD** 4 × 36 in (10 × 90 cm)
**POTTING MIX** Peat-free
**HARDINESS** Hardy to 34°F (1°C)
**SUN** ☼ ☼

The perfect foil for colorful flowers, this trailing plant is grown for its long stems of silver, heart-shaped foliage, rather than the small, yellow or white flowers that appear in early summer. It is drought-tolerant and easy to grow, and copes with some shade, too, though the foliage may lose a little silvery sparkle in these settings. Plant outside after the frosts, and trim the stems if they grow too long or you want to encourage bushier growth. A long drink once a week is all it needs to put on a dazzling show.

**The silver lace vine** 'Silver Falls' produces cascading stems of colorful foliage.

## KINGFISHER DAISY *FELICIA AMELLOIDES*

**HEIGHT AND SPREAD** up to 18 × 12 in (45 × 30 cm)
**POTTING MIX** Peat-free
**HARDINESS** Hardy to 23°F (−5°C)
**SUN** ☼ ☼

The bright blue daisies of this drought-resistant shrub make a colorful splash in a summer basket. The blooms balance on slim stems over small evergreen leaves and complement more brightly colored flowers in a mixed display. The kingfisher daisy will produce more blooms in full sun, but still offers plenty of flowers in light shade. Plant it outside after the frosts in a sheltered area, where it may overwinter and bloom the following year. Water twice a week and remove old flower stems.

**Kingfisher daisies** produce upright stems of small flowers from summer to fall.

## FUCHSIA *FUCHSIA* (SMALL SPECIES/CULTIVARS)

**HEIGHT AND SPREAD** 24 × 24 in (60 × 60 cm) or more
**POTTING MIX** Peat-free
**HARDINESS** Hardy from 34–14°F (1 to −10°C)
**SUN** ☼ ☼

Choose the compact forms of these versatile shrubs for a basket and also look out for hardy types that will perform year after year if overwintered in a sheltered spot. Fuchsia's dainty, often bicolored flowers hang like tiny ballerinas from arching stems, and appear through summer and early fall. Plant them outside after the frosts and water twice a week. Most fuchsias do not need deadheading, but cutting the flowering stems back lightly in late summer will help extend the show.

**The upright, hardy** *Fuchsia* 'Heidi Ann' makes a beautiful centerpiece in a basket.

## NEW GUINEA IMPATIENS

**IMPATIENS NEW GUINEA GROUP**

**HEIGHT AND SPREAD** up to 16 ×12 in (40 × 30 cm)
**POTTING MIX** Peat-free
**HARDINESS** Hardy to 50°F (10°C)
**SUN** ☼ ☀

Similar to the common impatiens (*Impatiens walleriana*) but larger and not prone to downy mildew disease, these robust plants create a striking centerpiece in a basket. The dark green leaves set off the round blooms, which come in colors from whites and purples to reds, oranges, and bicolors. They appear from summer to early fall and plants do not need deadheading. Plant out after the frosts in a sheltered spot.

**New Guinea impatiens** cope with some shade and bloom for many months.

## SENECIO JACOBAEA MARITIMA

**HEIGHT AND SPREAD** 12 × 12 in (30 × 30 cm)
**POTTING MIX** Peat-free
**HARDINESS** Hardy to 34°F (−10°C)
**SUN** ☼

The finely cut silver foliage of this drought-tolerant hardy perennial lends a lacy texture to basket displays of bright or pastel-colored flowers. The small yellow blooms can be removed if you don't like them—trim back the growing tips at the same time to encourage new bushy growth. Plant in full sun for the best silvery effects and water twice a week in spring and summer. Leave senecio *in situ* over winter, replacing the summer flowers with pansies and spring bulbs for cold-season interest.

**Formerly known** as *Senecio cineraria* 'Silver Dust', this plant earns its keep all year.

## NEMESIA NEMESIA

**HEIGHT AND SPREAD** 12 × 12 in (30 × 30 cm)
**POTTING MIX** Peat-free
**HARDINESS** Hardy to 23°F (−5°C)
**SUN** ☼ ☀

If you're looking for a tough, trouble-free plant that puts on a show from late spring to fall, add a nemesia to your shopping list. The dainty blooms come in a huge choice of colors and some cultivars, such as 'Wisley Vanilla', are sweetly scented. These plants do not need deadheading, but trimming back long stems as the season progresses will improve their performance. Plant them outside after the frosts; placed in a sheltered spot in the fall to overwinter, they may bloom again the following year.

**The perfect filler plants,** nemesias come in a wide choice of colors to suit any scheme.

## AFRICAN DAISY OSTEOSPERMUM JUCUNDUM

**HEIGHT AND SPREAD** up to 16 × 12 in (40 × 30 cm)
**POTTING MIX** Peat-free
**HARDINESS** Hardy to 23°F (−5°C)
**SUN** ☼

With daisy flowers in pink, white, purple, or yellow, these compact plants make a bold statement in a basket. One plant is all you need as a centerpiece, with a continuous display of flowers appearing from late spring to fall. Plant outside after the frosts in spring, and water well once or twice a week. Snipping off the old flower stems now and again will help keep plants looking neat. You can also overwinter them in a sheltered spot for a fresh bouquet of blooms the following year.

**White African daisies** create an elegant display in a basket and flower all summer.

## TRAILING GERANIUMS *PELARGONIUM PELTATUM*

**HEIGHT AND SPREAD** up to 12 × 16 in (30 × 40 cm)
**POTTING MIX** Peat-free
**HARDINESS** Hardy to 41°F (5°C)
**SUN** ☼

Also known as ivy-leaved geraniums, these plants are perfect for edging a basket, their trailing stems creating a veil of lobed leaves and colorful flowers. They are drought-tolerant and will need watering just once a week, or twice in hot summers. Plant them outside after the frosts in a sheltered sunny spot. For an extra sensory dimension, you could try a scented-leaf variety, such as *Pelargonium* 'Pink Capricorn', which has lemon-rose-scented foliage, bright pink flowers, and a slightly trailing habit.

**Trailing ivy-leaf geraniums** are named after their cascading stems of lobed leaves.

## VARIEGATED MINTLEAF *PLECTRANTHUS MADAGASCARIENSIS*

**HEIGHT AND SPREAD** 20 × 36 in (50 × 90 cm)
**POTTING MIX** Peat-free
**HARDINESS** Hardy to 41°F (5°C)
**SUN** ☼ ☼

This plant is grown mainly for its trailing stems of mint-scented, creamy-white and green leaves, which will cascade around the edge of a basket. Its small, pale blue, tubular flowers add to its charms in summer. Match it with white flowers to create a cool, sophisticated scheme or brighter blooms for a dazzling focal point. Plant mintleaf outside after the frosts in a sheltered spot, and trim the stems if they grow too long. It will need watering just once or twice a week to keep its foliage in good condition.

**An easygoing plant,** mintleaf creates a frill of colorful foliage around the edge of a basket.

## MONGOLIAN STONECROP *HYLOTELEPHIUM EWERSII*

**HEIGHT AND SPREAD** 6 × 8 in (15 × 20 cm)
**POTTING MIX** Peat-free
**HARDINESS** Fully hardy
**SUN** ☼

Drought-tolerant and easy to care for, this stonecrop produces trailing stems of gray-green, fleshy leaves that create a colorful contrast to summer bedding. In late summer, heads of tiny, bright pink flowers appear to add a final flourish to your display before fall. This plant is completely hardy, and although it loses its leaves in winter, they will reappear each spring. Water once or twice a week from spring to early fall and add a slow-release fertilizer each spring when new shoots emerge.

**This stonecrop's** gray foliage acts as a foil for its pink flowers, which appear in late summer.

## VERBENA *GLANDULARIA*

**HEIGHT AND SPREAD** 12 × 16 in (30 × 40 cm)
**POTTING MIX** Peat-free
**HARDINESS** Hardy to 23°F (−5°C)
**SUN** ☼

Not to be confused with the larger, hardier verbenas grown in the garden, bedding verbenas (*Glandularia*) are a great choice for a basket. From early summer until fall, they produce round heads of tiny blooms in a wide range of colors over a carpet of small green leaves. Use as a centerpiece or a filler around a taller plant such as a fuchsia. Water thoroughly twice a week. The occasional trim will keep plants healthy and flowering well. Verbenas may survive a mild winter if kept in a sheltered spot.

**Verbenas flower** in summer and early fall and may bloom again the following year.

# EASY CROPS FOR POTS

As well as herbs, most of which are well adapted to life in a pot, there are a few vegetables and fruits that will not require too much time or effort to grow in containers on a patio or windowsill. As with all potted plants, your edibles will need more effort than growing crops in the ground, but planting in containers can have some additional benefits. Raising edibles in pots set out of harm's way will help protect some plants that are susceptible to pests, such as slugs and snails, as well as providing the right site and soil conditions for those that require special treatment.

**Salad leaves are easy to grow** from seed and can provide up to three harvests from just one sowing.

## FRUITY POTS

**STRAWBERRIES** The best type of strawberry for growing in a pot is an everbearer that produces fruits in its first year from summer to early fall, but you can also select summer-fruiting varieties that have a shorter fruiting season if you prefer (see p.72). In spring, fill a large container at least 12 in (30 cm) wide and deep with commercial potting mix, and plant your runners (bare-root plants) so that the tops of the roots are buried, while the stems

and leaves are above the surface. Plant 3–4 strawberries in a 12 in (30 cm) pot.

Choose a sunny spot with a little shade at midday, if possible, and water your strawberry plants regularly so they never dry out.

Most potting mixes contain sufficient nutrients to sustain the plants for a few weeks, but as soon as the flowers appear, add a high potash fertilizer once every week or two. Harvest the fruits when they come away from the plant with a gentle pull.

Strawberry plants throw out long stems with little plantlets at the end, which you can remove or grow on into new plants. To grow them on, insert the base of the plantlet in a pot of potting mix and keep it watered. As soon as new shoots appear, sever the stem attached to the parent plant and grow on the young one.

**BLUEBERRIES** These delicious, vitamin-rich fruits are best grown in containers unless you have the acid soil (see p.12) they demand. Buy two plants, which are needed to cross-pollinate and produce a good crop, or select a self-fertile variety if you only have space for one. Choose a pot at least 12 in (30 cm) tall and wide and fill it with acidic growing mix. Plant the blueberry at the same depth as it was in its original pot and firm around it gently to remove large air pockets. Add a layer (mulch) of seasoned wood chips over the potting mix to help lock in moisture.

Site your plants in full sun or part shade, and water about twice a week in the growing season, ideally with rainwater. Nutrients in the potting mix will sustain the plants for a few weeks; add a fertilizer for acid-loving crops when the flowers appear. Harvest from mid- to late summer, depending on the variety. In spring, remove the top inch of potting mix and replace it to replenish nutrients.

**Everbearer strawberries** grow easily in containers and will produce sweet, juicy fruits all summer.

**Plant blueberries** in large containers filled with acidic growing mix and water about twice a week in summer.

**Cut your salad leaves** with scissors, but leave short stumps which will regrow to deliver a second crop.

**Harvest radishes in pots** when you see the little pink or red roots poking up above the potting mix.

**Spring onions** are quick and easy to grow in containers, with crops ready to harvest about 12 weeks after sowing.

# EASY VEGETABLES

**SALAD LEAVES** Growing salad leaves from seed in containers is easy, and you can sow small batches throughout the spring and summer for a long harvest. Alternatively, purchase small plug plants from a garden center or supermarket to pot up.

When buying seed, opt for loose-leaved cut-and-come-again types, rather than those that form a head, such as butter, romaine, or iceberg lettuces. Choose from packs of mixed seeds for a range of flavors or single varieties of your favorite leaves. The spicy Japanese salads mizuna and mibuna (see p.63) can also be grown as cut-and-come-again leaves.

Simply fill your container with commercial potting mix, use your palm or the bottom of a seed tray to gently create a smooth, even surface, then make shallow drills with a short bamboo cane. Sow the seed thinly into the drills, cover lightly with potting mix, and water using a can fitted with a rose head. Keep the pots

in a cool, partly shaded place on a table or old chair to protect the seedlings from slugs and snails. Water every other day, unless it rains, until the plants germinate, after which you can water a little less frequently—but never allow the potting mix to dry out completely, which may cause the plants to "bolt" (flower) and the leaves to turn bitter. When the seedlings are about 6–8 in (15–20 cm) in height, snip off the foliage with scissors to leave 1 in (2.5 cm) stumps. Keep watering and the stumps will then regrow. Repeat the process and you should get about three harvests from each sowing.

**RADISHES** These little flavor bombs are easy to grow in pots and will add some zing to your salad leaves. Follow the advice for sowing lettuce seeds but set your pots of crops in full sun in spring, then move them to part-shade in summer to prevent them bolting. These quick-maturing crops should be ready to harvest about 4–6 weeks after sowing when you see the little roots pushing out of the potting mix.

**SPRING ONIONS** Grown for their spicy flavor, these hardy little onions are very easy to grow in pots, either by sowing them from seed from spring to summer, or potting up young seedlings bought from the garden center.

If growing your onions from seed, fill a container with commercial potting mix, press it down gently, and make some shallow drills with a stick or short length of bamboo cane. Sprinkle the seed into the drills, cover them with ½ in (1 cm) of potting mix, and water gently, using a can fitted with a rose head. Keep the potting mix moist and seedlings will soon appear. Spring onions rarely need to be thinned, but take out any seedlings that look too congested. Your delicious onions should be ready to harvest about 12 weeks after sowing.

**TOP TIP** LETTUCES ARE COOL-SEASON CROPS AND THE SEED WILL NOT GERMINATE IN TEMPERATURES OVER 77°F (25°C), SO ONLY SOW WHEN COOLER CONDITIONS RETURN.

**Sustainable hardwood floors**
need no maintenance, apart from the
occasional sweep, while a simple stone
and wood bench will also need little care.

# FLOORS, WALLS, AND FURNISHINGS

Choosing materials for the floors and walls in an outdoor
space can be daunting when there are so many different
types on offer, but those that are long-lasting and require
no regular treatments are the best options if you want
to minimize maintenance. When selected carefully,
these products can be better for the environment, too.
Fortunately, furniture made from durable materials that
have a long life and are easy to clean can create beautiful
features for the dining and seating areas of your yard.

# LANDSCAPING MATERIALS

Any patio, deck, or path will need sweeping occasionally to remove dirt and debris, but your choice of materials can reduce other maintenance to a minimum. Their durability is a factor to consider, since poor-quality products will need to be replaced more frequently, adding to your workload and potentially increasing pollution if they are not recyclable and end up in landfill. Before buying, also think about how easy your hard surfaces will be to clean. Dirt that can be removed with a brush or water, rather than chemicals that may also damage your plants and the environment, will make life easier.

**Pavers in mottled colors** laid in a random pattern will not show the dirt as much as uniform light- or dark-colored paving.

## PAVING FOR PATIOS AND PATHS

Paving and bricks are durable and hard-wearing, which means you will not need to replace them for many years, while materials that do not show the dirt will also need cleaning less frequently. Try slabs that can be laid in a random pattern, and are either mottled or mixed pastel shades, which will not show the dirt as much as solid pale or dark colors. Many natural stone pavers and clay bricks have textured surfaces that can trap dirt, too, so choose a sawed and honed finish if you want your patio to sparkle. Also check your stone supplier's ethical policy to ensure child labor was not used in the quarry—locally sourced products may be the best choice and will have traveled fewer miles. Often cheaper than stone, smooth, concrete-based paving is fairly durable and easy to clean but it has a very high carbon footprint, while porcelain tiles, available in many finishes, are more eco-friendly.

Paving stones can be laid either on a rigid base of cement mortar or on loose sand over an aggregate base. So-called loose laying allows water to drain and prevents run-off and flooding, but the sand base will allow weeds to grow in the gaps. However, by filling the spaces with pretty plants, you can eliminate the problem (see pp.102–103).

**Softwood decking** is relatively inexpensive but may require treating with a preservative every year or two.

## DECKING OPTIONS

When choosing decking, a type made from softwood will probably be your cheapest option but it may need treating annually to prolong its life. A hardwood deck with FSC certification (see p.35) will probably be more expensive but could last a lifetime and requires no extra treatment. In shady areas where moss growth may make timber decking slippery, composite decks made from recycled plastics and wood offer a good solution. These materials do not suffer from moss or algal growth, and are nonslip and very easy to clean. They will last a lifetime, too, but because they are made from mixed materials they're currently difficult to recycle; choose carefully so yours won't need to be replaced.

**Well-built walls** made from clay or natural stone bricks provide an easy-care, sustainable boundary that will last a lifetime.

# WALLS, FENCES, AND SCREENS

A brick wall is one of the most enduring and beautiful boundaries for a space; if built well and from good-quality bricks, it should require little or no maintenance for many years.

When choosing fencing, cheap, softwood screens may seem like the best option, but they can be the most time-consuming to maintain and often blow down in the first gale that whistles through the yard. To prolong the life of softwood, you will need to apply a preservative every year or two.

Pressure-treated softwoods have a longer lifespan, but check that the chemicals used do not include creosote, copper, and permethrins, which are toxic to humans and the environment. Reclaimed softwood fencing panels and posts may also contain hazardous arsenic and chromium. Hardwood fences will last much longer with no treatments, so may be the best choice if they also display an FSC logo (see p.35).

Rustic woven hazel or willow hurdles are an option for temporary boundaries or screens. While they will need no treatment after installation, they only last for a few years, although many are fully biodegradable.

# OTHER MATERIALS

Most gravels do not show the dirt and make cost-effective and easy-to-lay informal paths and seating areas, but weeds may take hold in loose gravel, which can increase its maintenance.

When laid on a well-trodden path, however, the constant footfall drives out the air needed for weeds to germinate, reducing the problem.

A wood chip path is also easy and cheap to lay, and weeds will find it difficult to take hold in a layer 2 in (5 cm) deep—just remember to remove perennial weeds before you start. For larger spaces, try self-binding gravel, which is made up of aggregates in a range of particle sizes that create a weed-free, porous, and maintenance-free surface when compacted down.

**Self-binding gravel** offers a durable, permeable surface that requires very little maintenance, apart from sweeping.

# THE BIG CLEAN-UP

Most types of paving can be simply power-washed each spring to remove surface dirt. After that, it is up to you how much time you want to spend cleaning. A long-handled, stiff-bristled broom will sweep up debris and food quickly and efficiently from a patio or deck. Leave any uncontaminated muddy dirt to dry and then sweep the dusty particles into the borders or onto a lawn, running the brush over the grass to ensure that the dried mud settles between the leaves.

Do not use detergents, even those that the manufacturers claim to be gentle, where soapy water will drain into a water feature: it will increase algae and other weeds, while harming fish and wildlife. It may take a little longer, but scrubbing surfaces with plain warm water and a stiff brush is a safer option.

**A hose** on a powerful jet setting will lift off surface dirt from paving, but make sure it does not also remove cracked grout.

# PLANTING BETWEEN PAVING STONES

**Weeds that set seed between paving are a nuisance. They take time to remove by hand, while chemical weedkillers offer only a temporary solution and harm the environment (see pp.128–129). The low-maintenance answer is to cover the gaps between stones with ornamental plants that block the light and use up the nutrients that weeds need to thrive. The effect suits both contemporary and traditional designs.**

**Raised walkways** above dense planting and a pebble mulch will combine to keep most weeds at bay.

## CHOOSING A WEED CONTROL

One way to prevent weeds from growing between the cracks in your patios and paths is to fill them in with mortar. However, mortars and grouts are not permeable and as rainwater flows off hard surfaces, it can cause localized flooding elsewhere in the space. In addition, paving grout usually contains cement, which produces high levels of pollution during its manufacture. The natural solution is to fill the spaces with plants, which outcompete the weeds and prevent flooding. Some will also feed pollinators such as bees and butterflies.

**A gravel layer** between plants helps suppress weed growth as they establish.

**Chamomile** thrives in sunny spots and will withstand light foot traffic.

## PLANTS FOR PAVING CRACKS

Low-growing plants that produce a dense mat of roots and leafy stems are the best choices for filling the gaps between paving. Creeping herbs such as thyme and chamomile are ideal for sunny sites and, once planted, require very little maintenance. They also emit a soothing scent when the leaves are brushed. Both thyme and chamomile will survive some footfall, but like all other plants (including weeds) they may suffer on a main route through the yard. For a

**Aubrieta** produces colorful spring flowers and a mat of evergreen leaves.

flowery effect, try Mexican fleabane (*Erigeron karvinskianus*)—its leaves overwinter in sheltered spots and the little daisies bloom from spring to fall. Happiest in full sun, this tough little plant also grows well in partial shade. Aubrieta is another option for a sunny site and flowers profusely in spring; run a lawnmower on its highest setting over the plants after the blooms have faded to encourage bushy growth and a second flush of flowers. Mint-scented pennyroyal (*Mentha pulegium*) is a good choice for partly shaded areas, or you could use the blue star creeper (*Isotoma axillaris*) in mild regions.

# HOW TO PLANT
# A THYME PATH

**YOU WILL NEED** Crowbar or garden fork • Trowel • Peat-free potting mix • Your choice of thyme plants • Watering can or hose

1. In spring, use a trowel, fork, or crowbar (if needed) to lift some bricks or paving tiles along your path. Use a trowel to dig holes in the gaps to accommodate your thyme plants.
2. Plant bushier thyme species for fragrance and culinary use on the edges of the path, and low-growing ones such as creeping thyme more centrally. The crown of the plants (where the roots meet the stem) should be slightly lower than the pavers.
3. Fill in around the plant roots with potting mix and gently press it down to remove any large air gaps. Water well.
4. Water the plants during dry spells for the first couple of months until you see new growth appearing, after which they should not need any further irrigation. The thyme should spread between adjacent paving cracks to produce a weed-free barrier. Keep plants neat by trimming the stems after flowering.

## SOWING SEEDS

If paving cracks are too small to fit in a mature plant, sow some flower seeds into the gaps in spring. They should germinate within a few weeks and the plants will then help smother weeds. To sow Mexican fleabane and aubrieta seeds (see *opposite*), use a knife to extract some of the old grout and fill the cracks with potting mix. Sprinkle seeds on the potting mix but do not cover them, as they need light to germinate, then water lightly.

**Seeds of Mexican fleabane** (*Erigeron karvinskianus*) germinate in tiny cracks.

### NEED TO KNOW

- Do not use strong detergents to clean patios or paths that you have planted up—they may damage the plants and also enter and pollute underground water sources.
- Take care when power washing your surfaces, as the water pressure may lift out the roots of plants growing in the paving cracks.
- If plant stems become long and leggy, trim them after flowering to stimulate bushier growth and encourage more blooms.

# CARING FOR YOUR LAWN

A lush lawn creates a beautiful, practical feature but it comes at a price, in terms of both maintenance and its cost to the environment. Regular mowing, watering, weeding, and feeding can be quite a chore, while the use of fertilizers, herbicides, and gas-powered mowers contribute to high pollution levels. So, to keep maintenance and your carbon footprint low, try some of these simple lawn care tips.

**Frequent mowing** of the lawn and removal of the clippings is the most labor-intensive task in the summer.

## LET THE GRASS GROW

One easy way to reduce maintenance is simply to cut the lawn less frequently. As well as reducing your workload, this benefits the grass, too. Deeper roots grow to sustain the longer leaves, which in turn are more able to withstand longer periods of drought. Leaving the clippings in situ after mowing also helps the lawn thrive because they release nitrogen, a plant nutrient, as they decompose, which reduces the need for fertilizers to keep the grass green.

They also smother the soil between the blades of grass, which helps prevent weed seeds from germinating.

Reducing mowing frequency allows other plants to grow, including clover (see opposite) and wild flowers such as buttercups, daisies, plantain, and bird's foot trefoil (*Lotus corniculatus*) that provide food for pollinators and the caterpillars of butterflies. You can take this further and cut the grass and flowers just once or twice a year to create a perennial meadow that offers a home for wildlife (see p.106–107).

### NEED TO KNOW

Letting your grass grow for just a few months of the year could cut your mowing time in half. Mowing from midsummer until mid-fall will allow the spring flowers to bloom in the grass earlier in the year, while creating a short lawn during the summer months for play or sunbathing. Do not use weedkillers on the lawn, which will kill off the wildflowers.

**Allowing the flowers** to bloom in longer grass saves you time mowing and provides food for the bees and butterflies.

**Cutting the grass less frequently** reduces your workload while retaining the lawn as a soft play surface.

**Leaving daisies and clover** to grow in a lawn will decrease your workload while still producing a largely green surface.

**Programmable robotic mowers** take the work out of keeping a lawn neat.

## WILD ABOUT WEEDS

Tolerating some weed growth can be the best policy for a low-maintenance lawn. Mowing just once every few weeks will remove many of the weeds' flowers before they set seed and reduce the vigor of their leaves and stems, too, weakening their growth.

Encourage more clover to take root in your lawn or even grow it instead of grass (see p.109) as a way of reducing time spent on your lawn. While some may think of it as a weed, clover can in fact be the easy-care gardener's savior.

It is a legume and, like all plants in this group, it extracts nitrogen from the air to fuel its growth and that of the grasses growing close to it. This little plant out-competes many other weeds and its lush leaves tolerate footfall, although not as well as grass. To establish clover in a lawn, mow the grass in late spring and remove the clippings to expose the soil between the blades. Mix clover seeds with dry horticultural sand and scatter evenly over the lawn. Water frequently to keep the soil moist, and do not walk on the area for about two months until the clover is well established.

## GRASS ALTERNATIVES

If you are using your lawn as a decorative surface rather than for playing, relaxing, or walking on, there

are a number of low-growing plants you can use instead (see pp.108–109) that do not require mowing and can add a wildlife-friendly feature to the yard.

Alternatively, you may be tempted by artificial grass, which is laid on top of leveled soil like a carpet. While these tough, all-weather products are easy to maintain and clean with a brush and hose, they are essentially large pieces of nonbiodegradable plastic and other materials that are not easily recycled, so bear this in mind if you are looking for an eco-friendly alternative.

**Artificial grass** offers an easy-care, all-weather surface but it is made of polluting nonbiodegradable plastic.

## ROBOTIC POWER

If you want a neat and tidy lawn but have no time to mow it, a robotic mower could be the answer. These machines are battery-powered and guided by a boundary wire laid around the edge of the lawn. You can program them via an app or control pad on the machine and most mow every other day in the growing season, removing about ⅛ in (3 mm) each time and leaving the clippings to lie on the ground, which helps fertilize the grass. They then return to their dock to recharge once the task is complete. Their electric motors are quiet, too, and emit no air pollutants. All these benefits make them perfect for a low-maintenance yard, but they are expensive to buy and will also need an outdoor electricity supply, installed by a qualified electrician. The mower requires about 6 ft (2 m) of clear space around the docking station to maneuver, which may be impractical in a small space.

**TOP TIP** DO NOT WATER GRASS THAT HAS TURNED YELLOW DURING A DRY SUMMER; IT WILL SOON DEVELOP ITS GREEN COLOR AGAIN WHEN RAIN RETURNS.

# TURNING A LAWN INTO A MEADOW

**Lawns may be high maintenance, but a perennial meadow comprising grasses and wildflowers needs very little care once established. Meadows are easy to make from a patch of lawn if you're happy to exchange your green carpet for a more naturalistic feature, and thrive in similar conditions to mowed grass—but unlike a lawn, they won't need fertilizing and grow best in poor soils that contain few nutrients.**

**Simply allowing** your lawn to grow can produce a beautiful flower meadow filled with pollinator-friendly blooms.

**The wildflowers** in a perennial meadow appear year after year and are quite subtle in color.

## WHAT IS A PERENNIAL MEADOW?

Not all meadows are the same. Some thrive in wet soils and others include colorful annual plants, such as poppies and cornflowers, that are either resown each year or the soil is turned annually in the fall to promote self-seeding. The third type, known as "perennial meadows," are the easiest to make and manage and these include the plants that are mostly already present in your lawn, including greater knapweed, ox-eye daisies, clover, bird's-foot trefoil (*Lotus corniculatus*), buttercups, meadow cranesbill (*Geranium pratense*), and bush vetch (*Vicia sepium*), to name a few. Once established, the flowers in these meadows will pop up every year among the grasses with little effort from you.

## EASY SOLUTIONS

All you need to do to make a meadow from a lawn is to leave the grass to grow to its full height. The grasses may outperform the wildflowers for the first year or two, especially in soils that have been fertilized, but the meadow can still produce a beautiful effect as it rustles and sways. Once the soil fertility has been reduced, the flowers will start to gain ground, though you can achieve this effect faster by adding extra plants (see *opposite*). You can transform your whole lawn into meadow or just a section of it, mowing only the remainder to reduce your workload. Mowing a pathway through a large meadow will allow access through it, too.

**For the best of both worlds,** transform part of a large lawn into a meadow to reduce the area you need to mow.

# HOW TO ESTABLISH A MEADOW

The best time to establish a meadow from a lawn is in spring or early fall, but stop using fertilizers and weedkillers as soon as possible. You do not need to add more flowers if you are prepared to wait a couple years for the self-sown flowers in the lawn to establish.

**YOU WILL NEED** Trowel or small fork • Wildflower plug plants (optional) • Scythe or shears (optional) • Mower

1 Using a trowel or small fork, dig out pernicious weeds, such as dock and dandelions, including the roots. Then leave the lawn to grow uncut until the summer. Some wildflowers already in the grass mix will start to grow taller, too.
2 To achieve a flowery effect more quickly, in spring buy wildflowers from special suppliers as small seedling plants (plugs). The annual yellow rattle (*Rhinanthus minor*) is particularly useful because it helps reduce the vigor of the grasses, allowing more flowers to thrive. Remove small sections of turf and plant the plugs into these pockets.
3 After the flowers have bloomed and set seed in late summer, mow the meadow, leaving the grass no shorter than 2 in (5 cm)—you may need to use a scythe or shears to remove the long growth. Leave the cut stems *in situ* for a week or two to allow the seeds to disperse.
4 Remove and compost the meadow clippings. If left in place they will rot down and nourish the soil, resulting in more grass growth, which will out-compete the flowers.
5 Mow and remove the meadow clippings annually in late summer to maintain the balance of grasses and flowers. Do not water a meadow; the grasses and flowers are very drought-tolerant.

# LAWN ALTERNATIVES

If your aim is to cut the time spent tending a lawn while still retaining a low-growing leafy carpet, try one of these plants instead. They all produce decorative foliage and flowers and some will tolerate light footfall, too. However, unlike a lawn, they are not suitable as play surfaces, paths, or for a main route through the yard, where grass would still be your best option. Most of these plants are very drought-tolerant and rarely require watering or feeding, so pick one best suited to your conditions and just sit back and relax.

## CHAMOMILE *CHAMAEMELUM NOBILE*

**HEIGHT AND SPREAD** up to 10 × 24 in (25 × 60 cm)
**SOIL** Well drained
**HARDINESS** Fully hardy
**SUN** ☼ ☼

Chamomile has long been used as a lawn substitute; its ferny, aromatic leaves and white daisy summer flowers produce an attractive year-round carpet. This little plant only tolerates light foot traffic (do not walk on it in the first year after sowing), but it is relatively undemanding. Sow seed in spring or buy young plants, spacing them 6 in (15 cm) apart. Once established, trim the plants after flowering in late summer by running a mower over them on its highest setting to keep them neat and compact.

**Chamomile's** low-growing, ferny leaves release their sweet scent when crushed underfoot.

## SNOW-IN-SUMMER *CERASTIUM TOMENTOSUM*

**HEIGHT AND SPREAD** 6 × 24 in (15 × 60 cm)
**SOIL** Well drained
**HARDINESS** Fully hardy
**SUN** ☼

The spreading stems of this sun-loving perennial form dense mats of silvery evergreen foliage, which creates a beautiful lawn substitute in areas that are not walked on. In late spring and early summer, the foliage is studded with small white flowers with notched petals. It is extremely drought-tolerant and requires almost no care once established. The only task is to cut through the spreading roots with a sharp spade to remove plants that are creeping outside their designated area.

**Mats of silvery foliage** create a sparkling carpet decorated with dainty white flowers in spring and summer.

## SWEET WOODRUFF *GALIUM ODORATUM*

**HEIGHT AND SPREAD** 6 × 24 in (15 × 60 cm)
**SOIL** Any, except wet
**HARDINESS** Fully hardy
**SUN** ☼

Sweet woodruff is a great choice for a shady site, quickly covering the ground with its divided evergreen leaves— each one like a little star—and clusters of small white flowers from late spring to midsummer. All parts of the plant are sweetly scented, and while it won't like being walked on regularly it can withstand the occasional crush. Bees are attracted to the flowers, and both foliage and blooms can be used in potpourri. The roots will spread far and wide, so dig out unwanted sections in spring to keep it in check.

**Spreading to form a mat** of divided leaves, sweet woodruff bears small summer flowers

## SEDUM *SEDUM*

**HEIGHT AND SPREAD** 4 × 39 in (10 × 100 cm) on a mat
**SOIL** Well drained
**HARDINESS** Fully hardy
**SUN** ☼

Low-growing sedums are succulent plants with fleshy leaves suitable for an area that will not be walked on. The easiest way to install these lawn substitutes is to purchase a sedum mat, which comprises collections of low-growing sedum species that produce a tapestry of colorful leaves and flowers from spring to early fall. The plants are pre-grown on a fiber base that you simply lay over leveled, weed-free soil like a carpet. Water while establishing, after which the plants should cope unaided.

**Low-growing sedums** produce a colorful carpet of textured evergreen foliage.

## CREEPING THYME *THYMUS*

**HEIGHT AND SPREAD** up to 4 × 12 in (10 × 30 cm)
**SOIL** Well drained, alkaline or neutral
**HARDINESS** Fully hardy
**SUN** ☼

One of the best alternatives, creeping thymes not only produce scented leaves and pollinator-friendly summer flowers, they also withstand light foot traffic. Good choices are wild thyme (*Thymus serpyllum*) with its purple flowers; *Thymus* Coccineus Group, which produces pink blooms; and the pale pink-flowered woolly thyme (*Thymus polytrichus*). These drought-tolerant plants need almost no maintenance, but trimming them with shears after flowering will keep the stems neat and bushy.

**Creeping thymes** have fragrant leaves that make a beautiful decorative surface.

## BLUE MOOR GRASS *SESLERIA CAERULEA*

**HEIGHT AND SPREAD** up to 8 × 12 in (20 × 30 cm)
**SOIL** Well drained, alkaline or neutral
**HARDINESS** Fully hardy
**SUN** ☼ ☼

With its tufts of blue-green leaves and spikes of purplish spring flowers, this compact evergreen grass looks like a shaggy lawn when planted *en masse*, but unlike turf it does not need regular mowing. It will tolerate low levels of foot traffic but it is essentially a decorative plant. Rarely succumbing to any pests or diseases, it is also drought-tolerant once established, although it may need watering occasionally during prolonged periods of drought. Cut back tired-looking plants in spring to encourage new growth.

**Fountains of blue-green** leaves animate the yard when they sway in the breeze.

## WHITE CLOVER *TRIFOLIUM REPENS*

**HEIGHT AND SPREAD** up to 8 × 24 in (20 × 60 cm)
**SOIL** Well drained
**HARDINESS** Fully hardy
**SUN** ☼ ☼

White clover makes a good lawn alternative, its mats of round divided leaves withstanding some foot traffic, while the small white summer flowers attract bees. Choose a micro-clover with its smaller but tougher leaves and stems for areas of higher foot traffic. Sow the seed in spring on well-prepared soil and water regularly while the seedlings are establishing. Clover is drought-tolerant, requires no fertilizing, and will not need mowing unless you want shorter plants.

**Clover flowers** are very attractive to bees, so mow off the blooms in areas that will be walked on.

# GREEN ROOFS AND WALLS

**Greening a roof or wall has many benefits for gardeners looking for low-maintenance options. Well-chosen plants covering walls or fences can prolong the life of these structures, while green roofs help insulate buildings and create easy-care decorative features that can also provide homes for wildlife. Some walls and roofs are easier to care for than others, so consider the options before you start.**

**A sedum mat** is easy to install on a shed roof, adding color and increasing the biodiversity of a yard.

**Green roofs** include an assortment of different sedum species that produce flowers in succession over many months.

## GOING GREEN

Walls and fences covered with climbing plants create beautiful screens of leaves and flowers, and these plants are very easy to grow in any space, whatever its size. A green roof comprising tiny, drought-tolerant sedum plants may take some time and effort to install but, once established, largely takes caer of itself. As well as adding to the decorative value of a space, these green surfaces offer a range of environmental benefits, providing nesting sites for birds and habitats for pollinating insects, while absorbing carbon dioxide and other air pollutants responsible for global warming. They also help prevent water run-off and localized flooding.

## LIVING WALLS AND FENCES

The easiest way to green up your vertical surfaces is to grow easy-care climbers (see pp.52–55) over them. Check your chosen plant's climbing method and install an appropriate support such as wires or trellis before you start planting (see pp.50–51). Dig a large planting hole twice the width and about the same depth as the root ball, at least 18 in (45 cm) from the wall or fence. This gap is required because the area adjacent to a vertical surface is normally very dry and plants will struggle to establish there. Lean the stems toward their support, remove any tape or string attaching the stems to a cane and loosely tie them onto their support with soft twine. Finally, water the plant in well and keep watering during dry spells for the first year or two. Also check the maintenance needs of your plants, which may need to be pruned once a year.

**Virginia creeper (*Parthenocissus*)** makes a beautiful, leafy feature on a large wall or fence, but it can be too invasive for a house wall.

**A small pavilion** with a gently sloping roof is ideal for an easy-care sedum mat roof.

# EASY-CARE ROOFS

The best and easiest green roofs for low-maintenance gardens are pre-sown mats comprising a range of sedum plants, which offer evergreen foliage and flowers from spring to early fall. These are relatively easy to install on a shed, garage, or summerhouse with a flat or gently sloping roof, but if you want to cover a roof on your house, check first that you do not require planning permission, and call in professional landscapers to ensure it is safely and correctly installed.

Most matting for the domestic market is suitable for the average shed or summerhouse, but make sure that your roof is in good repair before you start and ask for advice from your suppliers if you are unsure about its load-bearing capacity. To prevent wind lifting off the mat, you will need to install a metal or timber edging that allows good drainage. The plants on these roofs also need at least six hours of sun every day to thrive.

To install a sedum mat, first apply a waterproofing layer such as thick polythene or pond butyl liner that fits the roof exactly. On a flat roof with a slope of 3° or less, you will also need to add a drainage mat on top, since sedum plants dislike soggy soil conditions—your suppliers will provide this. The matting is heavy, so make sure you have some help to lift it onto the roof. You then simply unroll it, ensuring there are no gaps between the sections, trim off the excess, and water the matting well. The sedums will require regular watering for about a month after installation but they should then take care of themselves, apart from an annual feed in spring with a slow-release granular fertilizer, and, very occasionally, watering during prolonged periods of drought.

> **TOP TIP** IN THE FALL, CHECK YOUR GREEN ROOF AND REMOVE ANY WEEDS, MOSS, AND GRASSES. ALSO CHECK THAT THE DRAINAGE HOLES IN THE EDGING ARE CLEAR TO PREVENT WATERLOGGING, WHICH WILL KILL THE SEDUM PLANTS.

# GREEN WALL PLANTING SYSTEMS

If you want a green wall in a site where there is no soil beneath it to plant a climber, you could opt for a living wall planting system. These include flexible pockets attached to a backing board, or rigid plastic planters that click together to form a wall. Avoid the soft pockets, which tend to be very small, drain freely, and dry out rapidly, especially when installed on a sunny wall. Although generally more expensive, the larger, rigid units fitted with an integral automatic watering system are the best option for low maintenance. With a few DIY skills, you can build these yourself, or ask the experts to install the system for you. A living wall will require more irrigation in full sun, so to reduce your water bills, install yours in part shade. Here, you can include easy-care plants such as ferns, sedges (*Carex* species, except *Carex pendula*), bugle (*Ajuga reptans*), trailing bellflowers (*Campanula poscharskyana*), and heucherellas.

**Installing a planting system** with automatic irrigation is the easiest way to achieve a lush green wall like this.

# LOW-MAINTENANCE FURNISHINGS

**Lunch on a patio or an afternoon spent lying in the sun are two of the best ways to enjoy your low-maintenance yard, but before buying furniture to create your outdoor retreat, check that it will not increase your workload. Choices include plastic furniture that is easy to clean, coated or treated metals that need just a little care, and timber pieces that can be both low maintenance and eco-friendly.**

**Modern sofas and chairs** made from synthetic materials are easy to maintain, but the cushions will need protection from heavy rain showers.

## CHOOSING FURNITURE

With so many elegant dining sets, weatherproof sofas, and beautiful benches to choose from, how do you know which will require the lowest maintenance? The longevity of your furniture is often a clue and this can be measured by the length of the manufacturers' guarantee. A short-term guarantee suggests that the furniture will not last very long, and you may have to apply preservatives to timber pieces or replace others that deteriorate quickly, costing you additional time and money. So, as a rule of thumb, opt for the

best-quality products you can afford. Remember that furniture made from synthetic materials, such as wicker-look sofas, can come with 20-year guarantees but they are nonbiodegradable and may end up in landfill when you are finished with them. So when selecting this type of furniture, think long-term; invest in timeless pieces that you can take with you if you move, and look for those made from recycled materials.

Timber furniture can be long-lasting and an eco-friendly choice, depending upon the type and how the wood was treated—toxic chemicals are sometimes used in pressure treatments (see p.101).

Hardwood furniture will last a lifetime without treatments, if you don't mind it fading to a silvery gray color, while untreated softwoods will need to be protected every year or two with a water-based preservative to prevent them from rotting. Whichever type of timber furniture you choose, check that it has FSC certification (see p.35) and is from a sustainably managed forest.

Metal furniture, apart from stainless steel and cast aluminum, can rust, so ask your supplier if it has been treated, and whether it will require any further maintenance when left out in the yard all year.

**You can treat hardwood furniture** with teak oil to retain its original color or leave it untreated to fade to silvery gray.

**Contemporary chairs** made from powder-coated metal are weatherproof and very easy to care for.

## SOFT SEATING

Many modern sofas and lounge seats have durable, weatherproof aluminum frames and plastic seats, making them almost maintenance free, apart from the occasional hosing to remove surface dirt. The cushions may be advertised as shower-resistant, but look more closely at the description and you may find that they should be kept under cover in a dry place when not in use. This means you will either need space to store them in your home over winter or to purchase a weatherproof cushion storage unit for the yard. Either way, moving cushions can be a bit of chore when heavy rain is forecast, so consider installing your

**Check for cushions** with removable covers that can be put in the washing machine to keep them clean.

furniture under an awning, a pergola with a roof, or a pavilion to protect them and save you hauling them around. Alternatively, opt for dining chairs and loungers with plastic mesh seats, which are often just as comfortable as cushions and can remain outside all year.

## LIGHTING THE WAY

Extending your enjoyment of the yard into the evening, lighting has become a must for a modern outdoor space. As well as illuminating seating and dining areas, it can also make the yard safer by lighting paths and steps. The choices range from state-of-the-art LED lighting systems, operated from a phone or touch pad, to a few candles placed strategically to light key areas. Solar lighting falls somewhere between these two extremes, and the latest models are easy to install, give off reasonable amounts of light, and cost nothing to run. Whichever type of lighting you choose, select good-quality units, which should last longer than cheaper models. Steer clear of solar lights in plastic casings or LEDs on strings made from low-grade materials—their price may be tempting, but they break easily and often go to the landfill.

**Professionally installed** outdoor lighting adds to the yard's ambience and can be controlled with a phone.

A bubble fountain is an easy way to introduce the sight and sound of water and attract wildlife into your yard with minimal maintenance.

# EASY-CARE
# WATER FEATURES

Water features can be relatively easy to maintain, especially if they include running water or a selection of aquatic plants to keep the water clear. Making a pond will take some effort initially, but once it is well established, you may only need to remove weeds once or twice a year. Smaller features such as half-barrel pools can also be easy to care for when filled with plants, while bubble fountains may just need topping up occasionally to keep the water flowing.

# WATER FEATURES

Water animates a space with reflective light and sound, while attracting a whole host of birds, insects, frogs, and other wildlife into the yard. Even tiny water features (see pp.122–125) will create drinking stations for creatures, and any planted pond will increase your yard's biodiversity. Features with fountains or running water can be easier to care for, since the movement helps prevent the growth of algae, while naturalistic ponds filled with water-loving plants are also less prone to weeds because these ornamentals deprive them of the nutrients they need.

**Wildlife ponds** filled with water-loving plants will create a balanced ecosystem that requires little intervention.

## NATURE-BASED MAINTENANCE

One of the easiest water features to maintain is a naturalistic pond filled with a variety of aquatic plants, which help keep the water clear. Check out reliable wildlife charity websites for guides on how to make a pond if you do not already have one, and site it so that part of the water surface is in shade. Locate your pond away from deciduous trees, which will deposit leaves in the water in the fall and pollute the pond as they rot down.

Include an area that is about 3 ft (1 m) deep in the center of the pond. This will prevent the water from warming up too much in summer, which can lead to algal growth. The deeper water will also allow pond creatures to sit out periods of cold weather below the ice if the pond freezes in winter. Ensure that at least one side slopes down to the water to allow creatures easy access. Fill your pond with marginal plants in the shallows around the edge, some oxygenating plants to help keep the water clear, and one or two deep-water aquatics such as water lilies (see pp.118–121 for pond plants). Most plants should be kept in baskets and planted in aquatic potting mix— never use potting mix intended for land-based plants, which has too many nutrients. Together with insects and pond creatures, the plants will eventually create an ecosystem that is self-regulating and easy to maintain.

**Include irises and water lilies** to partly shade the pond surface and keep the water cool, which will help reduce weed growth.

**Plant new plants** in pond baskets or bags filled with aquatic potting mix and add them to your pond in spring.

**TOP TIP** DO NOT ADD FISH TO YOUR WILDLIFE POND. THEY HAVE A VORACIOUS APPETITE FOR NEWT EGGS AND FROG SPAWN, AND CAN UPSET THE DELICATE NATURAL BALANCE THAT KEEPS WEEDS AT BAY AND THE WATER CLEAR.

## SEASONAL CARE TIPS

In spring, add barley straw pads to help reduce algal growth, and introduce new plants from mid-spring. In summer, you may have to fish out excess duckweed (small round leaves on the surface) and algae from time to time—leave it on the side of the pond for a day or two in order to allow any pond creatures in it to return to the water. Top up your pond during hot weather with rainwater, or leave tap water in a bucket for a day or two before adding it to allow the chlorine to dissipate.

In the fall, remove barley pads that have turned black. In small ponds, use a net to remove leaves that have fallen in the water from nearby trees, or cover the whole pond with netting to trap them, making sure that you still allow pond creatures easy access. In winter, if your pond freezes, place a pan of hot water on the surface to melt the ice and provide water for birds and animals.

**Fish out duckweed** with a net when it threatens to cover the surface and place it on the side of the pond for a day or two so pond creatures can return home.

**After planting** your bog garden, water in the plants well and keep watering regularly until they are well-established.

## CONVERTING A POND TO A BOG GARDEN

If you have a pond but want to make a safer water feature for small children, convert it into a bog garden, which will be easy to maintain and will also increase the biodiversity in your yard. Drain your pond first, and if you have a butyl or plastic liner, use a garden fork to puncture a few holes in it. Break up a natural clay-lined pond in one or two areas to provide some drainage. Cover the liner or base with a 3 in (8 cm) layer of gravel or coarse sand and fill the pond with a mixture of garden soil (or imported topsoil) and well-rotted manure or garden compost. If your pond is deep, try half-filling it to create a sunken garden. Add a few cans of rainwater to the soil and leave to drain. Then plant up your feature with bog plants, adding a mulch (thick layer) of organic matter around the stems. A sunken garden should collect plenty of water to sustain these moisture-loving plants when it rains, but top up the water levels using a garden hose or stored rainwater during prolonged periods of drought.

**Fill your bog garden** with colorful moisture-loving plants such as water irises and primulas.

## PLANTS FOR A BOG GARDEN

Joe Pye weed (*Eupatorium purpureum*) • Meadowsweet (*Filipendula ulmaria*) • Water avens (*Geum rivale*) • Japanese water iris (*Iris ensata*) • Leopard plant (*Ligularia* species) • Gooseneck loosestrife (*Lysimachia clethroides*) • Ostrich fern (*Matteuccia struthiopteris*) • Bee's primrose (*Primula beesiana*) • Candelabra primula (*Primula japonica*) • Rodgersia (*Rodgersia* species)

# PLANTS FOR A POND

You can create a beautiful feature by planting up a small or medium-size pond with a collection of water-loving plants. This selection includes plants that will remain reasonably compact while providing a range of benefits to wildlife, and all are easy to grow. Including a few in your pool will also help keep the water clear and reduce weed growth. Take note of the pond depths given here, which are the measurements from the top of the root ball to the water surface and show each plant's preferred position in a pond or water feature.

## FLOWERING RUSH *BUTOMUS UMBELLATUS*

**HEIGHT AND SPREAD** up to 36 × 24 in (90 × 60 cm)
**POND DEPTH** 2–6 in (5–15 cm)
**HARDINESS** Hardy to 5°F (−15°C)
**SUN** ☀

This British native adds a delicate quality to the edge of a pond, with its airy sprays of small, pink, late-summer flowers held on long, slim stems. The blooms of this perennial attract pollinating insects and emerge from clumps of unusual three-sided leaves, which offer cover for frogs and other pond creatures. It thrives in the shallows of a pond or in a bog garden (see p.117). This rush is quite tall, so make sure it does not overshadow smaller sun-loving plants.

**The flowering rush** produces dainty sprays of tiny pink flowers that draw in pollinating insects to feed on the nectar and pollen.

## MARSH MARIGOLD *CALTHA PALUSTRIS*

**HEIGHT AND SPREAD** 24 × 18 in (60 × 45 cm)
**POND DEPTH** 0–¾ in (0–2 cm)
**HARDINESS** Fully hardy
**SUN** ☀ ☀

The large buttercup-like flowers of the perennial marsh marigold, or kingcup as it is also known, bring a cheerful note in late spring and provide a feast for pollinating insects. It is a well-behaved marginal or bog plant that rarely outgrows its allotted space and will be happiest with the top of its root ball just below or at the water surface. The foliage fades in summer and can look tattered after flowering, so use other plants to cover it or cut the stems back and new growth will emerge.

**The sunny yellow** buttercup blooms of the marsh marigold brighten up a pond in spring.

## CUCKOO FLOWER *CARDAMINE PRATENSIS*

**HEIGHT AND SPREAD** 18 × 12 in (45 × 30 cm)
**POND DEPTH** 0–¾ in (0–2 cm)
**HARDINESS** Fully hardy
**SUN** ☀ ☀

Dainty clusters of lilac-pink, purple, or white flowers appear in late spring or early summer on this perennial marginal or bog plant. The green divided foliage adds to its charms and creates a decorative frill around the shallow edges of a pond. The cuckoo flower, or lady's smock as it is also known, is easy to grow and relatively well behaved, but it may need lifting and dividing every few years when it outgrows its basket. It may also self-seed into other damp areas of the yard.

**This marginal plant** bears pale pink flowers from late spring as the cuckoos arrive.

## HORNWORT *CERATOPHYLLUM DEMERSUM*

**HEIGHT AND SPREAD** 1 × 5 ft (30 × 150 cm)
**POND DEPTH** 6–18 in (15–45 cm)
**HARDINESS** Fully hardy
**SUN** ☼ ☼

Hornwort may have little decorative value, but this fernlike oxygenator plays an important role in the welfare of your pond. It releases oxygen into the water, aiding the growth of plants, insects, and other wildlife, while sopping up nutrients that weeds need to grow, thereby helping to keep the water clear. It's sold in bundles, and you simply untie the stems and throw them into the pond. Allow it to cover about 30 percent of your pond, then remove excess growth in summer.

**Hornwort** is an oxygenator that will grow unaided in your pond and helps to keep the water clear.

## BLUE FLAG *IRIS VERSICOLOR*

**HEIGHT AND SPREAD** 30 × 30 in (75 × 75 cm)
**POND DEPTH** 2 in (5 cm)
**HARDINESS** Fully hardy
**SUN** ☼ ☼

The blue flag is a well-behaved water iris that produces a profusion of small, blue-purple or reddish-purple flowers in early summer. It will attract pollinating insects to its flowers, and other water wildlife will hide among its leaves. Ideal for a small pond, this pretty marginal should be planted in shallow water. Although it will create a good-size clump, it's not as vigorous as the Japanese iris and does not need dividing as frequently. Like its cousins, the blue flag needs no other attention once planted.

**The variety 'Kermesina'** produces red-purple flowers with yellow and white veining.

## JAPANESE IRIS *IRIS LAEVIGATA*

**HEIGHT AND SPREAD** 12 × 36 in (30 × 90 cm)
**POND DEPTH** 4–6 in (10–15 cm)
**HARDINESS** Fully hardy
**SUN** ☼ ☼

One of the easiest irises to grow, this species has long, sword-shaped leaves and blue or purple flowers that appear in late spring or early summer. It will soon fill a basket, so if you want a large clump, plant it in a big container that will provide space for its roots to spread. You will need to lift and divide it every few years in spring, but it needs no other attention. The foliage offers a great hiding place for frogs and other water creatures. 'Variegata' is not as fast-growing as the species plant.

**'Variegata'** has purple flowers and white-striped leaves for additional interest.

## WATER FORGET-ME-NOT *MYOSOTIS SCORPIOIDES*

**HEIGHT AND SPREAD** 12 × 24 in (30 × 60 cm)
**POND DEPTH** 0–4 in (0–10 cm)
**HARDINESS** Fully hardy
**SUN** ☼ ☼

Creating a sea of tiny blue flowers among simple green leaves at the water's edge, this charming perennial is hard to resist. Bees, butterflies, and other pollinators are also attracted to the dainty blooms. Very easy to grow, it will soon fill a basket, so plant it in a large container if you want a good-size clump. You will then need to divide the plants every few years to contain their spread. They may self-seed into other damp areas of the yard, but unwanted seedlings are easy to pull up by hand.

**Water forget-me-not** bears tiny blue flowers in spring, just like its land-based cousin.

# WATER LILY 'LAYDEKERI LILACEA'

*NYMPHAEA* 'LAYDEKERI LILACEA'

**SPREAD** 18 in (45 cm)
**POND DEPTH** 6–10 in (15–25 cm)
**HARDINESS** Hardy to 5°F (−15°C)
**SUN** ☼

One of the best water lilies for a small pond, the flowers of 'Laydekeri Lilacea' are pale pink when they open, then change to darker pink. The glossy foliage features brown blotches. Set water lily plants on bricks initially, so their foliage floats on the surface, and gradually remove the supports as the stems grow. Push a water lily fertilizer into the potting mix in spring—you may have to wade into the water to do this.

**This lilac-pink** water lily is perfect for a small pond and produces fragrant blooms throughout the summer months.

# WATER LILY 'MARLIACEA CARNEA'

*NYMPHAEA* 'MARLIACEA CARNEA'

**SPREAD** 4 ft (1.2 m)
**POND DEPTH** 2–3 ft (60–90 cm)
**HARDINESS** Hardy to 5°F (−15°C)
**SUN** ☼

Grown for its vanilla-scented, semi-double, pale pink flowers, this beautiful water lily is a good choice for a medium-size pond. Blooming from summer to early fall, it may produce white flowers in its first year. Its dark green leaves provide shade, keeping the water cool for aquatic creatures and helping to prevent algae. Planting and care is the same as for 'Laydekeri Lilacea' (see *left*).

**'Marliacea Carnea'**, like all water lilies, prefers still water, so do not plant it near a fountain or tumbling cascade.

# WATER LILY 'ODORATA SULPHUREA'

*NYMPHAEA* 'ODORATA SULPHUREA'

**SPREAD** 30 in (75 cm)
**POND DEPTH** 12–24 in (30–60 cm)
**HARDINESS** Hardy to 5°F (−15°C)
**SUN** ☼ ☼

The brown and maroon mottled foliage of 'Odorata Sulphurea' adds an extra layer of color beneath the pale yellow, star-shaped flowers that appear throughout summer. Despite its name, the blooms are only lightly scented. A good choice for a small pond, it also tolerates light shade. Its care is the same as for 'Laydekeri Lilacea' (see *above*). If you want an even smaller yellow water lily, try *N*. 'Pygmaea Helvola'.

**'Odorata Sulphurea'** produces star-shaped yellow flowers with many petals that give them a distinctive look.

# PICKEREL RUSH *PONTEDERIA CORDATA*

**HEIGHT AND SPREAD** 4 × 2 ft (1.2 m × 60 cm)
**POND DEPTH** 12 in (30 cm)
**HARDINESS** Hardy to 5°F (−15°C)
**SUN** ☼

Pickerel rush is an elegant marginal perennial that produces large, spear-shaped leaves that create a decorative feature in themselves, even before the spikes of small, pale blue flowers appear in late summer. Ideal as a centerpiece in a small pool or part of a collection of plants in a bigger pond, pickerel rush should be grown in a large basket to allow its roots to spread. You will need to lift and divide it every few years when it outgrows its container, but it will generally take care of itself after planting.

**Handsome foliage** and spikes of pale blue flowers make a winning combination.

## MARSH CINQUEFOIL *POTENTILLA PALUSTRIS*

**HEIGHT AND SPREAD** up to 16 × 16 in (40 × 40 cm)
**POND DEPTH** 4 in (10 cm)
**HARDINESS** Fully hardy
**SUN** ☼ ◐

Marsh cinquefoil, or bog strawberry as it is also known, is a quietly beautiful plant, with upright stems of gray-green leaves divided into small leaflets, and loose clusters of dark red, star-shaped flowers, which appear in early summer. It is a good choice for a small pond or barrel pool and an excellent plant for pollinators, especially bumblebees. Slow-growing and trouble-free, it rarely requires maintenance after planting, although you may have to divide it when it finally outgrows its basket.

**Dainty star-shaped** flowers and strawberry-like divided leaves will adorn a small pond.

## WATER CROWFOOT *RANUNCULUS AQUATILIS*

**HEIGHT AND SPREAD** 4 × 24 in (10 × 60 cm)
**POND DEPTH** 10–24 in (25–60 cm)
**HARDINESS** Fully hardy
**SUN** ☼

The common water crowfoot is an aquatic perennial with submerged, feathery leaves and lobed, floating leaves that sit on the surface of the water. In late spring and summer, the foliage is joined by white flowers that look like little stars sprinkled over the pond. Like hornwort, it is an oxygenator (see p.119) and helps to keep the water clear. Grow it in a basket in a small pond to prevent it spreading too far, and divide every few years. It is happy in both still and running water.

**Small white flowers** appear in profusion for many weeks on this deep-water aquatic plant.

## LESSER SPEARWORT *RANUNCULUS FLAMMULA*

**HEIGHT AND SPREAD** 12 × 24 in (30 × 60 cm)
**POND DEPTH** 0–¾ in (0–2 cm)
**HARDINESS** Fully hardy
**SUN** ☼

Dotted with yellow summer flowers that look like those of buttercups, this dainty plant makes a great habitat for aquatic creatures. Water beetles, frogs, and toads living in the shallows will shelter among its dense stems of spear-shaped leaves, while pollinators such as bees are attracted to the flowers. Although lesser spearwort is prone to self-seeding in other damp areas of the yard, any unwanted plants are easy to remove. It is an easy-going species and requires little maintenance after planting.

**Nestling at the edges** of a pond, lesser spearwort will attract bees to its little flowers.

## MINIATURE CATTAIL *TYPHA MINIMA*

**HEIGHT AND SPREAD** 24 × 18 in (60 × 45 cm)
**POND DEPTH** 4–12 in (10–30 cm)
**HARDINESS** Fully hardy
**SUN** ☼ ◐

Unlike the common cattail (*Typha latifolia*), which should only be planted in large-scale ponds, this miniature form is perfect for a small garden feature or a barrel pool. In summer, its slim, grassy stems develop round, blackish-brown "maces," which are a type of catkin. Grow it in a basket at the edge of a pond in shallow or slightly deeper water, as it is not too fussy. It requires almost no attention after planting but will need to be lifted and divided after a few years when it has outgrown its basket.

**This tiny cattail** makes an eye-catching addition to a small pond, or a barrel or patio pool.

# SMALL PATIO POOLS

A small pool for a patio or courtyard reflects light into your space and draws in birds and other wildlife, even in a tiny area. Adding some plants helps to keep the water weed-free and clear, while baskets or pots provide landing stations for frogs and birds that come to take a drink or bathe. These little ponds are very easy to set up and should take only a few hours to install.

**A half barrel** makes a beautiful patio pool and will accommodate a range of easy-care plants to attract wildlife.

## CHOOSING AND SITING A PATIO POOL

Select a watertight container that is at least 12 in (30 cm) wide and deep—the bigger the better, as the presence of more plants will help regulate the water temperature and limit weed growth. A watertight half barrel is ideal for a patio feature, but check before you buy that it has not contained toxic liquids—a traditional beer or whiskey barrel would be perfect, or one bought from a nursery and designed for garden use. Some traditional oak barrels may leak at first but will become watertight as the wood swells, so fill yours and wait for a few days. If it still leaks, you will have to add a pond liner. Line the barrel, add water, which will push the lining into place, and tack it at the top with round-headed stainless steel nails.

Glazed, frost-proof containers without drainage holes also make beautiful features for patios. If yours has a hole in the bottom, try plugging it with a wine cork or add a pond liner or sheet of recycled plastic to make it watertight. The water and plant baskets will help keep the liner in place.

Tiny pools will heat up very quickly, so set yours in part shade, choose plants that are happy in cooler conditions, and keep the water topped up.

> **TOP TIP** BEFORE PLANTING UP, SET YOUR BARREL OR POT WHERE YOU INTEND TO KEEP IT BECAUSE IT WILL BE VERY DIFFICULT TO MOVE ONCE FULL OF WATER AND PLANTS.

**Site small patio pools** in part shade so the sun does not heat up the water too quickly and accelerate weed growth.

**Divide water lilies** and other pond plants that have outgrown their baskets by using a knife to slice through the roots.

## POTTING ON

After a couple of years, some of the plants in your mini pond may outgrow their baskets and need to be divided or planted in a larger container. In spring, remove the plant from its basket: the roots will have grown through the holes, so you will need to carefully cut the plastic container with a sharp knife or scissors to extract the plant. Then, using a sharp knife, slice through the root ball and repot a healthy section in a new basket of the same size, or plant it up in a larger basket that will accommodate it (see *opposite for planting instructions*). You can give away the unwanted sections or compost them, but never dispose of pond plants in another water source without prior permission.

# HOW TO MAKE A
# CONTAINER POOL

**YOU WILL NEED** Frost-proof glazed
container • Stiff brush • Wine cork
(optional) • Pond baskets • Aquatic
potting mix • Selection of compact
pond plants (*see below*) • Gravel •
Colander or sieve

1 Clean the inside of the container with
  a stiff brush and rinse with fresh water.
  Do not use soap or detergent, which
  will pollute the water. If your pot has
  a drainage hole, use a wine cork to
  make it watertight. Fill the container
  with water to about 2 in (5 cm) below
  the rim using rainwater or, if using
  water from the tap, leave it for a day
  or two before planting to allow the
  chlorine to dissipate.

2 Choose a pond basket with small
  holes in the sides. Add a layer of
  aquatic potting mix to the base.
  Carefully remove your pond plant
  from its original container and place
  it in the center of the basket. Fill in
  around the plant with more aquatic
  potting mix, gently firming it down to
  remove large air gaps. Wipe off any
  duckweed or algae on the leaves of
  the plant with a clean cloth.

3 Place some gravel in a colander or
  sieve, and rinse it a few times under
  a tap to remove dust and impurities.
  Apply a ¾-in (2-cm) layer on top of
  the potting mix to help prevent it from
  escaping and muddying the water.

4 Add the basket to the glazed pot. Do
  not worry if the leaves of a water lily
  are submerged at this stage—they
  will soon float to the top. If planting
  marginals that prefer shallow water,
  stand them on stones or bricks to
  raise their baskets to the correct
  pond depth (see their plant labels for
  this information). Add about three
  plants to a container 18 in (45 cm)
  wide. Scoop out pond weeds with
  a small net from time to time.

## AQUATIC PLANTS FOR
## A PATIO POOL

Marsh marigold (*Caltha palustris*)
• Miniature water lilies (*Nymphaea
odorata* var. *minor, Nymphaea*
'Pygmaea Helvola' and 'Pygmaea
Rubra', and *Nymphaea tetragona* are
all good choices) • Blue flag (*Iris
versicolor*) • Japanese water iris
(*Iris ensata*) • Slender club rush
(*Isolepis cernua*) • Corkscrew rush
(*Juncus effusus* f. *spiralis*)

***Iris ensata* 'Rose Queen'** is a
compact marginal ideal for a patio pool,
producing pink flowers in summer.

# EASY-CARE FOUNTAIN FEATURES

Bringing a dynamic energy to any space, moving water features such as bubbling fountains or water blades are also easy to maintain. Some may require professional installation, others can be assembled from kits, while "plug in and go" features just require an electricity supply or solar power to pump the water through them. These features will all need an annual clean but require little care apart from that.

**A cascading water blade** makes a dramatic statement in a modern garden and needs just a little annual care.

## CHOOSING A FEATURE

There are many different types of fountain feature on the market, ranging from small, solar-powered units to cascading water blades that create a stylish, contemporary look. Budget can be a determining factor, since a blade or wall-mounted fountainhead may require professional installation unless you have very good DIY skills, but once set up, they then don't need much maintenance (see *opposite*). If you have an outdoor electricity supply, you can plug in a fountain feature and enjoy it all year, or buy one with a solar-powered pump and a backup rechargeable battery, which will run on overcast days and evenings but probably not in winter. These features usually have a long cable attachment so you can place the solar unit in the sun and the fountain in part shade, where the water will not evaporate as quickly in summer. Whichever type you choose, look for a good-quality feature with a long-term guarantee, or you may find it only works for a year or two before breaking and ending up in the landfill.

**Solar-powered patio features** are very easy to install, cost nothing to run, and take just an hour or two to clean.

The reservoir beneath this bubbling feature is buried in the ground and disguised with gravel and pebbles.

## INSTALLING BUBBLE FOUNTAINS

Bubble fountains all work in a similar way, with a "sump" (reservoir) to hold the water, and a pump that pushes it up through a fountainhead, from where it runs back down into the reservoir in a continuous cycle. If you buy a kit, the sump will comprise either a vessel that you bury in the ground or, with smaller features, a bowl-like unit that sits on a patio and may need to be disguised with planting or ornaments.

Large or tall features may require an outdoor electricity supply, rather than a solar-powered pump, since most domestic units do not have sufficient power to push the water very far. When installing a permanent feature, locate it in part shade and away from deciduous trees that will drop their leaves in the fall. Also think about how you will conceal the reservoir—a layer of gravel or pebbles, or both, works well on buried units and helps prevent the holes that allow water to drain back into it from clogging up with soil or garden debris. They also help to keep the reservoir cool, which will reduce evaporation rates and the need to top it up with water as frequently.

### NEED TO KNOW

- Sterilizing tablets are sometimes added to the water in small or large fountain features to keep it clear. However, the chemicals in them can leach into the soil and pollute waterways when they filter down into the groundwater.

- Constantly moving water will help prevent algae from forming on fountains and blades, but any that does grow can be cleaned off with a cloth or brush and tap water. Don't use detergents, which are pollutants.
- Avoid using abrasive cleaners on stainless steel features.

## MAINTENANCE TIPS

Remove any leaves, twigs, and other garden debris from the water in a fountain every few weeks, since these may clog up the mechanism. Also, clean solar panels and check them periodically for cracks or damage, and top up the water reservoir every week during warm or windy weather. During the summer, use tap water to clean skimmers, strainers, and filters that are attached to the pump, or ask your installation company if it offers a maintenance service to keep your fountain in good working condition.

In temperate climates, you can keep your fountain or bubble feature on throughout winter, when the moving water will prevent it from icing up. If you are not planning on using your fountain or you live in a cold area, drain your feature, remove all pumps, fountainheads, and filters, and store them indoors. Cover your feature to keep out the elements or take it indoors for the winter.

In midsummer, remove the pump from your fountain and clean it carefully with a hose or rinse it in the kitchen sink.

**Watering young and establishing** plants is essential, but placing pots close to an outdoor tap will cut the time and effort needed for this task.

# GARDENING MAINTENANCE

All outdoor spaces need a little pampering now and again to keep them looking their best, but there are ways to make sure that the workload doesn't become a burden. Watering can be reduced by giving plants enough to drink each time and by using automatic systems. Pruning is easy when you know how, and few plants need to be cut more than once a year, while nipping pests and diseases in the bud before the problem spreads can also help minimize maintenance.

# WEED OUT THE WORK

Once weeds start to spread they can be tough to eradicate. Weeding is laborious and time-consuming, so prevention is always better than cure. The way to reduce your workload is to inhibit weed seed germination and block the path of these plants' spreading roots. Start by identifying the weeds that recur year after year so you can readily recognize their seedlings, which are much easier to remove than mature plants.

**Apply weed-suppressing** landscape fabric beneath a layer of gravel to prevent weed growth between sun-loving plants.

## COVER THE SOIL

Weeds are adapted to spread quickly. Their flowers produce thousands of seeds, which can fly into your yard on the breeze or be distributed by birds, springing into life as soon as they land on bare soil. An easy way to reduce germination rates is to cover exposed soil with a 2in (5cm) layer of homemade compost, well-rotted manure, wood chips, or gravel—known as a mulch—which blocks the light that weeds need to grow and prevents them from taking root in the ground. Weed-suppressing landscape fabric performs a similar role, creating a barrier over the soil surface. Some weeds may still germinate on organic mulches, such as compost or manure, but they are easy to hoe off or pull out because their roots do not establish well on these loose materials.

**Ornamental plants** can produce a beautiful blanket over the soil surface that leaves no space or light for weeds to take hold.

**Lay a mulch** over the soil between your plants to prevent weed seeds germinating.

## FILL THE GAPS

In the same way that mulches prevent weed seeds from germinating, covering the soil with a dense blanket of ornamental plants is another highly effective way to prevent their growth. Pack your plants in tightly so they create a dense, leafy canopy that shades the soil surface, reducing the light that weed seeds require. Your plants will also use up the water and nutrients that allow weeds to thrive. A few dandelions and other weeds may pop up during the spring in the gaps between perennial plants as their new growth emerges, but a couple of hoeing sessions should keep seedlings at bay.

**Push the blade** of a Dutch hoe just beneath the surface to sever weeds' top growth from the roots.

## HOEING HINTS

Small, annual weed seedlings are easy to remove with a hoe, and even perennial types that form long tap roots, such as dandelions, will find it difficult to survive hoeing when they are young. This technique also allows you to remove weeds without digging. Use a Dutch hoe to sever the top growth from the roots by pushing the blade back and forth just beneath the soil surface. To reduce your workload, hoe in dry, sunny conditions when you can simply leave the weeds to shrivel on the surface. Hoeing can also create a "dust mulch," a layer of loose soil in which weed seeds cannot easily germinate.

**TOP TIP** TRY NOT TO DISTURB THE SOIL BY DIGGING, WHICH BRINGS BURIED WEED SEEDS UP TO THE SURFACE WHERE THEY WILL THEN GERMINATE. DIG ONLY TO PLANT NEW PLANTS, REMOVE PERNICIOUS WEEDS, OR CREATE A VERTICAL WEED BARRIER.

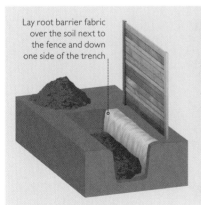

Lay root barrier fabric over the soil next to the fence and down one side of the trench

**Create a vertical barrier** to prevent weed roots from invading your yard from neighboring sites.

## ROOT OUT THE PROBLEM

Some pernicious weeds spread via their roots, which can creep under fences from neighboring properties to colonize your space. To prevent these invaders from moving in, dig a narrow trench 18 in (45 cm) deep along your boundary and install a vertical barrier made from paving slabs or a root-barrier fabric that the weeds cannot penetrate. Refill the trench with the excavated soil. Vertical barriers may not prevent all weeds from migrating but they will reduce the problem.

## TAKING OUT TOUGH WEEDS

Perennial weeds such as dandelions, bindweed, brambles, horsetails, and ground elder are tough plants that are difficult to eradicate once they become established. Using chemical weedkillers is not recommended because they harm the environment, and most are ineffective in the long term. For example, bindweed has an extensive root system that domestic weedkillers rarely kill completely.

The best solution for large weed-infested areas is to cut back the plants' top growth and cover them with old carpet or recycled black plastic sheeting, making sure that no light can reach the remaining stumps or the surrounding soil. Keeping this in place for about a year should kill the weeds. Alternatively, keep an eye on affected areas and cut down all of the weeds' stems to the ground as soon as you see them, which will weaken the plants and help keep them at bay. For individual weeds, try digging out the whole plant, including all the roots, since they will regrow from even a tiny piece of root.

**Cover areas** infested with bindweed with old carpet or plastic sheeting to block the light it needs to grow.

# MINIMIZING WATERING

Watering is one of the main jobs in any yard, but your plant choices and soil preparation will help reduce this task. Once established, most mature plants can tap into water sources deep in the ground and, if you have chosen species that enjoy the conditions in your yard, they will survive on rain alone. However, any new or young plants, and those in pots and baskets, will require your attention.

**Minimize wastage** by soaking the soil over a plant's roots rather than watering the leaves or flowers.

**Laying a mulch** and a drip hose over the soil will both deliver and trap sufficient moisture to enable young shrubs to establish well.

## EASY ACCESS

Mulching will help the soil retain moisture, but this may not be sufficient to sustain the growth of young plants or those in pots. You will still need to irrigate these plants, and, if you choose to water by hand, the task will be easier when you have a water supply close by. An outside tap is extremely helpful, but it will not be possible to site all beds and containers next to it, so install rain barrels on structures such as a shed or summerhouse to widen your range. Barrels not only provide free rainwater, which most plants prefer, they also help prevent localized flooding by capturing rain that would otherwise flow into overloaded drainage systems.

**Install rain barrels** next to a greenhouse and other buildings to provide water stations close to your plants.

## PREPARE THE GROUND

As well as selecting plants that enjoy your site and soil conditions (see pp.12–13 and 20–21), which should thrive with little intervention once established, add a mulch to the soil surface to lock in moisture. In warm or windy weather, water quickly evaporates from the soil, but a 2-in (5-cm) layer of organic matter such as leaf mold or well-rotted garden compost or manure spread over the surface will form a protective barrier that traps the moisture below. Ensure these mulches do not touch the stems of shrubs and trees, and if you are growing Mediterranean-style plants such as lavender and rock roses, use a layer of gravel or aggregates instead, which will keep their roots moist and their stems dry. Lay your mulch after a heavy downpour in the fall on clay soils or in spring on light, sandy soil or loam. If no rain falls, irrigate and then lay the mulch.

## SLOWLY DOES IT

The best way to water plants in beds and borders is with a seep or drip hose. These leaky hoses slowly release water into the soil with almost no wastage and can be laid around your plants and then covered with a mulch to reduce evaporation even further. Attach the hoses to an outdoor tap or a rain barrel and you can then regulate watering manually or install a programmable timer (see below) to irrigate your plants at preset times.

**TOP TIP** IRRIGATE YOUR PLANTS IN THE EARLY MORNING OR LATE EVENING WHEN EVAPORATION RATES ARE LOW AND THE MOISTURE HAS TIME TO DRAIN DOWN TO ROOT LEVEL.

**Lay drip hoses** between young seedlings in a vegetable bed and water in the early morning or evening.

## WHEN NOT TO WATER

Before reaching for the hose or watering can on hot summer days, remember that most mature plants will be able to cope unaided. Established trees and shrubs are adapted to withstand periods of drought and you will rarely need to water them. Most perennials, if planted in the right conditions, are also resilient; if you see their leaves drooping at midday they may simply be conserving their water reserves and will often return to normal by the evening. However, if they are still wilting when the temperatures cool, give them a long drink. Target the water over the root balls—irrigating bare soil between plants is both wasteful and encourages weed growth.

## AUTOMATIC WATERING SYSTEMS

If you have no time to spend watering a newly planted bed or set of potted plants that need regular irrigation, an automatic watering system offers the perfect solution. These systems comprise a battery-operated timer to attach to an outside tap and a pipe that can be connected either to a drip or seep hose laid on a bed or border (see above), or to a series of drippers, which you insert in the ground near vulnerable plants or into pots and baskets. The least expensive kits are programmed manually, while more sophisticated systems allow you to control the watering timing and frequency from an app on your phone. Some systems can even measure the outside temperature, light intensity, and soil moisture, so they only irrigate your plants when they need it most, helping conserve water supplies.

**An automatic timer** affixed to an outside tap allows you to program your watering times and frequency.

**NEED TO KNOW**
When watering, give your plants a long drink each time. Water pots and containers until you see some liquid collecting on the surface. For new plantings in the ground, give each one about half a large watering can or the equivalent if watering with a hose. Water will then seep down to the lower depths of the pot or soil, and the plant roots will follow it. You will then only need to water every few days, saving you precious time.

**An established garden** filled with mature trees and plants will rarely need watering unless a severe drought occurs.

# FEEDING OPTIONS

Many mature plants grown in garden soil will rarely, if ever, need additional fertilizer, especially if you lay a mulch of organic matter over the soil each year. Plants in pots and those you have just planted may require some additional nutrients, as will some annual crops, such as tomatoes, squashes, and other fruiting edibles. The latest research also shows that feeding less often not only saves time but can actually have a beneficial effect on the nutritional value of the crops we grow, and many plants will thrive with less fertilizer than was previously thought.

**An organic mulch** will release its nutrients gradually to feed plants' roots throughout the growing season.

## WHICH PLANTS NEED FEEDING?

When you look at the natural world, you will see communities of trees, shrubs, grasses, and other plants thriving with no human intervention or applications of fertilizer. This is because worms and tiny microorganisms such as fungi and bacteria work to recycle the nutrients in the leaves that drop in fall, the bodies of dead creatures, and animal droppings above and below the ground, delivering them back to the plants' roots. While few domestic gardens recreate a natural ecosystem, research into garden soil shows that nutrient deficiencies are very rare and most mature plants will thrive without extra fertilizer, especially if you have matched your choices to your soil conditions (see pp.12–13 and 20–21). So, only apply fertilizers to young plants, those showing signs of distress, fruiting crops, and plants in pots.

Most fertilizers are applied in spring or summer because plants' growth rates slow in the fall and may stop altogether over winter, so no extra nutrients are needed during these seasons. When applying a fertilizer, make sure you follow the manufacturer's instructions.

**Limit the use** of artificial fertilizers on plants in the ground, since any excess may leach into and pollute groundwater.

## TOO MUCH OF A GOOD THING

Overfeeding plants is more detrimental than underfeeding, which is music to the ears of the low-maintenance gardener. In a container, too much food can cause the plant to leach nutrients in a process known as "reverse osmosis," so do not apply any more than the recommended dose, even if your plants look in need of extra care. Overfeeding is also harmful to the environment, because fertilizers that leach from the soil or potting mix often end up seeping into groundwater and polluting waterways such as rivers and oceans.

**Established perennials and bulbs** will not need extra fertilizers since most garden soils contain sufficient nutrients to sustain them.

## PLANTS IN POTS

Most commercial potting mixes contain nutrients to sustain the growth of plants for the first few weeks after planting. You can then top them up, if your flowers or crops look in need of extra nutrients, by adding a slow-release fertilizer to the potting mix, or two or three doses of a liquid seaweed feed, given a few weeks apart in summer.

For long-term plantings in containers, feed your plants in the spring with a slow-release balanced granular fertilizer, either derived from organic sources or a synthetic fertilizer. These will deliver a balance of the key plant nutrients nitrogen, phosphorous, and potassium (also known as potash) to sustain good growth throughout the year. Carefully remove the top layer of potting mix, ensuring you do not damage the roots, apply the fertilizer combined with some fresh potting mix, then water well.

**Liquid seaweed fertilizer** gives plants in pots a nutrient boost after the fertilizer in the potting mix has been absorbed.

## FERTILIZING CROPS

Most annual crops, such as leafy salads, spinach, and radishes, will not need any extra fertilizer other than an annual mulch of organic matter (see pp.58–59) applied to the soil. Fruiting plants, such as squashes, peppers, and strawberries, may need extra potassium (potash) as their flowers appear, especially when grown in pots. This nutrient supports good flower and fruit production and it is also given to flagging annual bedding plants in late summer to prolong flowering. Use a fertilizer formulated for tomatoes and apply it about once a fortnight as the fruits develop. New research shows that the nutrient content of many fruits increases when they are slightly stressed and fed less frequently, so you may wish to experiment with a longer gap between applications, which will, of course, also reduce your workload.

## FEEDING SICKLY PLANTS

The leaves of plants that prefer acidic soil conditions may start to turn yellow if the soil or potting mix is too alkaline. If so, you can add a tonic for acid-loving plants, but also consider replacing them with something more suited to your soil. Discolored leaves can be a sign of drought stress rather than a nutrient deficiency, so try watering your plants well to see if this improves their health.

**Apply a tonic** for acid-loving plants, such as this *Fatsia japonica*, if the leaves turn yellow.

### NEED TO KNOW

- One way to give young plants a good start is to add mycorrhizal fungi, available in granules, to the soil when planting (except when planting brassica crops such as radishes, mizuna, and mibuna, which the fungi cannot colonize).
- These naturally occurring fungi form a symbiotic relationship with plants, attaching to the roots then extending far wider into the soil. The fungi extract nutrients and water from the soil and deliver them to the plant, encouraging healthy growth in exchange for sugars from the plant host that fuel their growth.
- Encouraging these fungal networks will reduce the need to fertilize your plants.
- Avoid using fungicides, which kill these beneficial microorganisms.

**Apply a high potash fertilizer** to fruiting crops such as strawberries when the flowers appear.

> **TOP TIP** A 2-IN (5-CM) LAYER OF WELL-ROTTED MANURE OR GARDEN COMPOST LAID OVER THE SOIL SURFACE (A MULCH) HELPS IMPROVE THE SOIL STRUCTURE, MAKING THE PLANT NUTRIENTS ALREADY IN IT MORE AVAILABLE TO YOUR PLANTS.

# SIMPLE PRUNING TIPS

Buying woody plants such as shrubs and trees that fit the space you have allocated for them will reduce the need to prune them, but even well-behaved plants could need a little intervention from time to time to keep them healthy. Some perennial plants will also need to be cut back once a year, usually in spring, to make way for new growth. Using clean, sharp cutting tools makes these pruning jobs quicker and easier, and pruning correctly also reduces the chance of diseases entering the wounds.

**When removing branches** from a tree, make a few cuts to reduce their weight before cutting about 2 in (5 cm) from the main trunk.

## WHEN TO PRUNE

You should prune most spring-flowering shrubs and climbers just after they have finished flowering, and cut back those that bloom later in early spring. This is because early-flowering shrubs develop their flower buds on stems produced the year before they bloom, while later-flowering plants develop buds on stems that they have produced in the same year. Some plants, including buddleias and late-flowering clematis, should be cut back hard in spring to encourage more flowering stems, while others, such as mophead hydrangeas, are best pruned lightly.

Most trees should be pruned when they are dormant in winter. Some, such as birch (*Betula*), hornbeam (*Carpinus*), and magnolia, will bleed sap if you cut them from late winter to mid-spring, so prune at any other time of year. Cut back *Prunus* trees, including cherries and plums, in summer to avoid silver leaf disease. Before planning any major restorative work, make sure no power lines or telephone cables are in the way.

Not all plants like the same pruning treatment, so take a few minutes to research each of yours to discover how and when to prune them correctly.

**Prune mophead hydrangeas in spring,** cutting the stems down to the first or second healthy bud.

## HOW TO PRUNE

Always wear sturdy gloves when pruning and work with clean, sharp cutting tools. Use hand pruners for stems the width of a pencil or smaller, and a pruning saw or anvil loppers for larger stems—ratchet loppers will make the job easier. Ask a friend to hold your ladder steady if you need to prune tall stems, but call in a professional tree surgeon or arboriculturalist to cut large branches from trees or shrubs above head height or to carry out major restorative work.

You need to make pruning cuts quite precisely to keep the plant healthy. If your plant has individual buds (raised bumps or small shoots) located along the stem, make a slanting cut just above one of them, so that rain will drain away from it. If the buds are in pairs directly opposite one another, make a straight cut just above them.

Start by taking out dead and diseased stems at the base of the plant or cut them back to healthy wood. Remove

**On stems with alternate buds,** make a slanting cut just above one so that rain will drain away from the emerging stem.

stems that are crossing and rubbing against each other, which can create wounds open to infections. Then prune stems to keep them to the desired size or to encourage more flowering shoots.

## CUTTING BACK PERENNIALS

The top growth of perennial plants (see pp.20–21) can wither and die back completely over winter, or the stems and seed heads may dry out but remain standing. In the latter case, leave the plants to decorate the garden and provide hibernating sites for beneficial insects during the colder months, and then cut them back in early spring to allow room for new growth to push through. Use hedge clippers for large stands of plants or hand pruners for smaller groups. You can chop the clippings into smaller sections and leave them on the surface to make an instant mulch that will help protect the soil.

**In early spring,** make way for new growth by cutting back perennials with overwintering seed heads.

## DEADHEADING

Cutting off the dead or dying flowers of perennials and some shrubs can encourage the plant to produce more blooms, extending the display. You can simply pinch or snip off the flowers on plants with soft stems, or, for those with woody stems such as roses, use hand pruners to remove the whole flower head, cutting it just above a bud. Plants will survive and bloom again without this treatment, but if you have time, it can be worth deadheading every week or two.

Bulbs will only flower once each year, but they can still benefit from deadheading, which prevents them from putting energy into making seed rather than bulking up the bulbs below ground. These provide the food the plants need to put on a good show the following year.

**Removing faded flowers** every week or two will encourage plants such as dianthus to produce more blooms.

**TOP TIP** LOOK FOR BEDDING PLANTS SUCH AS SURFINIAS THAT ARE DESCRIBED AS "SELF-CLEANING." THIS MEANS THAT THEY PRODUCE A CONTINUOUS DISPLAY OF FLOWERS WITHOUT THE NEED TO DEADHEAD THEM.

# DEALING WITH PESTS

Insects and mollusks that munch on flowers or crops are present in every garden, but you can help reduce the damage they cause by growing plants resistant to attack, or luring an army of pest predators to keep their numbers in check. Also consider just how perfect your garden needs to be and perhaps tolerate some minor damage, rather than using chemical controls, which may harm the environment.

**Check under pots** in sheds and garages for snails hiding in the darkness before dining out on your plants as night falls.

**Seedlings** are more vulnerable to pest damage than mature plants, so protect them while they are young.

## PREVENTION FIRST

One of the easiest ways to minimize pest damage is to ensure your plants are healthy and growing vigorously—giving them the conditions they require will make them more resistant to attack. Seedlings and young plants are especially vulnerable to pests, so provide extra protection by growing them under cover or on a raised surface such as a table, where slugs and snails will not be able to reach them as easily. Choosing plants that are rarely troubled by pests, such as those listed in this book, will also reduce your workload.

## BRING IN YOUR ALLIES

In an ideal world, your yard's ecosystem should include finely balanced populations of pests and their predators. While this is rarely possible in reality, attracting birds, frogs, toads, hoverflies, and ladybugs will help protect your prized plants. Birds such as blackbirds and thrushes eat snails, while sparrows feed on slugs. Frogs and toads also enjoy a meal of mollusks, and these creatures will all visit your yard if you provide a water source such as a small pond (see pp.116–117 and 123–124).

Other allies include hoverfly and lacewing larvae that prey on aphids, and both ladybug larvae and adults, which will also keep these sap-suckers at bay. You can attract hoverflies and lacewings into the yard with pollen-rich plants, and ladybugs will fly in when aphid populations are on the rise.

**Ladybugs and their larvae** protect plants by consuming vast numbers of sap-sucking aphids each day.

**Check plants regularly** and wash aphids off rose buds and other tender shoots with a hose.

## CONTROLLING ATTACKS

Inspect plants that are susceptible to pest attacks every couple of days, and remove the offenders by picking off mollusks or removing aphids with a jet of water from a hose. Pest hunts do take time but may save plants from infestations and reduce your work or the loss of your plants later on. For example, removing aphids regularly from rose buds will prevent a problem as the flowers open.

Biological controls can also offer eco-friendly, effective control. The most popular are nematodes, which are microscopic creatures that eat a range of pests, and parasitic wasps that consume aphids. You buy them in packs, which you can store in a refrigerator until you're ready to use them, and then simply water them onto affected plants.

# COMMON PESTS

## ANTS
These insects actually do little harm to plants, although their nests can be a nuisance in pots. They can lead you to aphid infestations if you see them busy on your plants, since they feed off the sweet residue that aphids deposit.

## APHIDS
The scourge of many plants, aphids include greenfly and blackfly. They suck the sap from buds and stems, distorting and sometimes killing their host plants. You can remove them with a jet of water, use a tissue to wipe them off, or try biological controls.

## EARWIGS
These beetle-like creatures with pincers on their hindquarters snack on the flowers and leaves of clematis, dahlias, and chrysanthemums. Try trapping them in upturned flowerpots filled with dry grass and set on sticks close to vulnerable plants.

## LILY BEETLES
The pretty red color of these beetles belies the damage they do to lilies and fritillarias. Both adults and their black excrement-coated grubs eat foliage and buds. Check lilies every day or two, pick off the beetles, and wipe off their larvae.

## SLUGS AND SNAILS
A familiar sight in any yard, these slimy creatures can reduce plants to stubs in just a few hours. They prefer young, tender stems and leaves and will often leave older plants alone, so try to protect plants when they are vulnerable by keeping them out of harm's way indoors or on a table until the stems have toughened up. Protect other plants by setting slug traps, laying sand or eggshells around the stems, or using slug pellets based on iron phosphate. These may not be quite as effective as the blue metaldehyde pellets that are now banned in some countries, but they do not harm other wildlife or damage the environment.

## VINE WEEVILS
Adults are slow-moving beetles that make U-shaped holes in the leaves of a variety of plants but do little damage. However, their larvae eat roots and can quickly kill a plant. Pick off the adults or use biological controls to keep the grubs at bay. Also try inserting the bases of affected plants into fresh soil and the roots may regrow.

**Ants** may lead you to aphid infestations.

**Aphids** suck the sap from plants.

**Earwigs** love to dine on dahlia flowers.

**Lily beetles** and their grubs can kill lilies.

**Slugs** feed on a wide range of plants.

**Vine weevil** grubs do the most damage.

# PREVENTING PLANT DISEASES

Healthy plants are less vulnerable to diseases, so minimize the risks by making sure that yours are thriving. If a plant looks sickly, check the symptoms to ensure that it is not just lacking water or nutrients before assuming a disease has taken hold, since both can cause wilting and discolored leaves. When a disease does strike, removing affected parts quickly can sometimes allow plants to recover.

**Watering the soil** rather than wetting plants' leaves will help prevent some fungal diseases such as mildews.

## HEALTH CHECKS

Just like humans, plants are more prone to diseases if they are in poor health, so make sure yours are receiving the moisture, nutrients, and sunlight they need. Check new plants for signs of diseases before planting them in the garden, where they may infect others. Look at the leaves, stems, and flowers, and dry bulbs such as tulips for fungal growth or discoloration; unusual streaked flower or leaf colors can be signs of a virus or disease. Also, tip the plant out of its pot and check that the roots look healthy. If you do spot a disease, most nurseries will take back infected plants that are still in their pots.

**Gently tip new plants** out of their pots to check that the roots look pale cream or white and healthy.

## PREVENTING PROBLEMS

Some fungal diseases such as rust and black spot on roses spread through the spores on contaminated leaves lying on the soil, so if your plant is suffering from these conditions, pick up the infected material as soon as you see it and either bury it about 4 in (10 cm) below the soil or place it in a green waste recycling bin with a lid.

Chemical cures such as fungicides should only be used as a last resort, since they can damage the environment and kill beneficial fungi in the soil that help plants grow and remain healthy. Remember, too, that not all diseases are fatal, and some are best tolerated if they have little effect on the plant's overall growth or productivity. Powdery mildew on squashes, for example, does not seem to greatly reduce the crop or cause the plants too much harm.

Other diseases such as blight and some mildews can be fatal, so you may need to remove the affected plant, bag it up, and throw it away or take it to a local recycling site where it will be composted at high temperatures that kill pathogens.

**Squashes** often succumb to powdery mildew disease, but if kept in check by regular watering, it rarely affects the crop.

# COMMON DISEASES

### BLACK SPOT
Purple or black spots appear on the leaves of roses and other plants, which then turn yellow and fall, reducing the plant's vigor. Trash affected leaves that fall on the soil and remove stems with black markings in spring. Tolerate mild infections if your roses still flower well.

### BLIGHT
Potatoes and tomatoes are susceptible to this fungal disease, which ruins the crops. In potatoes, the leaves start to decay and turn brown, while the tubers turn reddish-brown and rot. The symptoms on tomato leaves are similar, and brown patches also appear on the fruits, which then decay rapidly. There is no cure for blight, but growing tomatoes in a greenhouse can protect them from the airborne spores, while early potatoes are not affected as much as later crops, since the disease usually strikes later in the summer.

### CLEMATIS WILT
Large-flowered hybrid clematis that bloom in early summer are most prone to this fungal disease; spring-flowering and later-flowering species are generally unaffected. The leaves develop dark spots, while the leaf stalks turn black and the stems then wilt and die off. Plant susceptible clematis with the root ball 2 in (5 cm) below the soil level. If it does then succumb, you can cut back all the affected stems to the ground and healthy young shoots should appear from the base.

### DOWNY MILDEW
This common fungal disease causes pale green, yellow, purple, or brown blotches on the upper leaf surfaces, and a fungal growth on the undersides. Severely diseased plants can also be stunted. Pick off and throw away affected leaves and increase the air circulation around the plants to prevent further infection. Water the soil only, ideally in the mornings, trying to keep the leaves dry as you do so.

### POWDERY MILDEW
This silvery-white fungus affects the leaves, flowers, and fruits of many plants suffering in dry soil. Remove any affected stems as soon as you see them, and trash fallen infected leaves in the fall to reduce infectious spores the following spring. Also, increase the air circulation around plants and water the soil but keep the leaves dry.

### RUST
Orange or yellow pustules on the undersides of the leaves indicate rust disease. Avoid nitrogen fertilizers, which encourage the growth of soft, lush leaves that are most vulnerable, and trash affected foliage in the fall to avoid spores overwintering. In many cases, rust does not severely affect plant growth.

**Black spot** can defoliate affected plants.

**Blight** causes leaves and crops to rot.

**Clematis wilt** is not always fatal.

**Downy mildew** causes leaves to rot.

**Powdery mildew** affects many plants.

**Rust** is caused by fungal spores in the air.

# INDEX

**Bold** text indicates a main entry for the subject.

**Author** Zia Allaway

## AUTHOR ACKNOWLEDGMENTS

Many thanks to Marek Walisiewicz at Cobalt id for commissioning me to write this book and to Paul Reid for his inspirational designs. Thanks also to editor Diana Vowles, and Amy Slack and Ruth O'Rourke at Dorling Kindersley for their help in focusing my ideas and fine-tuning the words.

## PUBLISHER ACKNOWLEDGMENTS

DK would like to thank Mary-Clare Jerram for developing the original concept; John Tullock for consulting; Margaret McCormack for indexing; and Paul Reid, Marek Walisiewicz, and the Cobalt team for their hard work in putting this book together.

## PICTURE CREDITS

The publisher would like to thank the following for their kind permission to reproduce their photographs:

**Alamy Stock Photo:** A Garden 9bl; Ammentorp Photography 23bl; Andi Edwards 137cl; Andreas von Einsiedel 10tr; Anne Gilbert 107br; Annie Eagle 108bl; Avalon.red 43bl; Bailey-Cooper Photography 130br; BIOSPHOTO 71cr; blickwinkel 54bl; Dave Bevan 12cr; Deborah Vernon 138br; Derek Harris 79tr, 110cl, 117cr; Ellen Rooney 18tr; Gavin Dronfield 106cl; GFK-Flora 109bl; Ingrid Balabanova 72br; John Gollop 14tr; Mim Friday 50bl; Nigel Cattlin 70bl; Oleksandr Sokolenko 92br; Panther Media GmbH 105tr; Paul Hobart 135bl; Pavol Klimek 51tr; Photiconix 51tr; Rebecca Erol 94tl; Ros Crosland 16c, 20tr; Sabena Jane Blackbird 119br; Simon Dack 124br; SOPA Images Limited 112tr; Steve Taylor ARPS 121bl; STUART WALKER 110br; Tim Gainey 46tr; TMI 63tl; Valentyn Volkov 76tr; Yon Marsh Pipdesigns 105tl; Zoonar GmbH 38tr.

**Dorling Kindersley:** 123RF.com: Yuliia Sonsedska 104bl; Alan Buckingham 72bl, 73br, 135tc, 139c; Bethany Dawn 104br; Brian North / RHS Chelsea Flower Show 2009 40bc; Brian North / RHS Chelsea Flower Show 2010 15tr, 112bl, 112br; Brian North / RHS Chelsea Flower Show 2011 2c, 12tr; Brian North / RHS Hampton Court Flower Show 2010 8tr, 101bl; Brian North / RHS Hampton Court Flower Show 2012 9tl, 40tr; Brian North / Waterperry Gardens 10cl, 28br; Dreamstime.com: Alexander Sidyakov 46bl; Dreamstime.com: Dmitri Maruta 119tl; Dreamstime.com: Sarah2 137br; Getty RF: mikroman6 136bc; iStock: PeopleImages 18cl; John Glover / Cambridge Botanic Gardens 29tr; John Glover / Royal Botanic Gardens, Kew 89bl; John Glover / Savill Garden, Windsor 88br; Mark Winwood / Alpine Garden Society 48tr, 81bl; Mark Winwood / Ball Colegrave 19bl, 82bl, 82br, 83tl, 83bl, 84tl, 85bl, 92tr, 92bl, 94br, 95br; Mark Winwood / Crug Farm 54bl; Mark Winwood / Dr Mackenzie 87tr; Mark Winwood / Hampton Court Flower Show 2014 30tr, 84tr, 93bl; Mark Winwood / RHS Chelsea Flower Show 2014 26bl, 33tl, 33br, 37bl, 46tl, 47bl; Mark Winwood / RHS Malvern Flower Show 2014 85tr, 93br, 102cr; Mark Winwood / RHS Wisley 19bc, 19br, 20cl, 20br, 26br, 28tl, 28bl, 29tl, 30tl, 30bl, 30br, 31tl, 31bl, 32bl, 32br, 38bl, 39br, 42br, 47tr, 49tl, 49tr, 52tr, 77tr, 80br, 81tl, 81br, 82tr, 84br, 85br, 86tr, 86bl, 89tr, 95bl, 103bc, 120tl, 120tr, 120bl, 137bc; Peter Anderson 21tr, 42tr, 45tl, 100l, 109tl, 113tr; Peter Anderson / RHS Chelsea Flower Show 2009 37br, 76br, 102c, 132bl; Peter Anderson / RHS Chelsea Flower Show 2011 51bl, 128cr; Peter Anderson / RHS Hampton Court Flower Show 64tl, 106br; Peter Anderson / RHS Hampton Court Flower Show 2009 67tr, 102tr, 110tr; Peter Anderson / RHS Hampton Court Flower Show 2010 64tr;Peter Anderson / RHS Hampton Court Flower Show 2014 21tl.

**GAP Photos:** 24br, 74c, 122tr; Clive Nichols - Design: Charlotte Rowe 113bl; Howard Rice 11tr; J S Sira - Designer: Ian Hammond. Sponsors: Squires Garden 111br; John Glover 114c; Mark Winwood 13tr; Michael King 50tr; Nicola Stocken 4c, 77br, 97tl; Visions 122cr.

**Getty Images:** Kelly Mitchell 100cr.

Illustrations by Cobalt id.

All other images © Dorling Kindersley

**Produced for DK by COBALT ID**

**Managing Editor** Marek Walisiewicz
**Editor** Diana Vowles
**Managing Art Editor** Paul Reid
**Art Editor** Darren Bland

**DK LONDON**

**Project Editor** Amy Slack
**US Editor** Megan Douglass
**Managing Editor** Ruth O'Rourke
**Managing Art Editors** Christine Keilty, Marianne Markham
**Production Editor** David Almond
**Senior Production Controller** Stephanie McConnell
**Jacket Designers** Nicola Powling, Amy Cox
**Jacket Coordinator** Lucy Philpott
**Consultant Gardening Publisher** Chris Young
**Art Director** Maxine Pedliham
**Publishers** Katie Cowan

First American Edition, 2022
Published in the United States by DK Publishing
1450 Broadway, Suite 801, New York, NY 10018

A catalog record for this book
is available from the Library of Congress.
ISBN 978-0-7440-4812-4

DK books are available at special discounts when purchased in bulk for sales promotions, premiums, fund-raising, or educational use. For details, contact:
DK Publishing Special Markets, 1450 Broadway, Suite 801, New York, NY 10018
SpecialSales@dk.com

Printed and bound in China

### For the curious
www.dk.com